TIPTOEING THROUGH HELL

TIPTOEING THROUGH HELL

PLAYING THE U.S. OPEN
ON GOLF'S MOST
TREACHEROUS COURSES

JOHN STREGE

HarperCollins*Publishers*

HarperCollins books may be purchased for educational, business, or sales promotional use. For information, please write: Special Markets Department, HarperCollins Publishers Inc., 10 East 53rd Street, New York, NY 10022.

FIRST EDITION

Designed by Peng and Nancy Olaguera

Printed on acid-free paper

Library of Congress Cataloging-in-Publication Data

Strege, John.
    Tiptoeing through hell : playing the U.S. Open on America's most treacherous courses / John Strege.— 1st ed.
        p.   cm.
    ISBN 0-06-018864-2
    1. U.S. Open (Golf tournament)—History.   2. Golf courses—United States.   I. Title.

GV970.3.U69 S77   2002
796.352'66—dc21

                                                            2001051814

02 03 04 05 06 WB/RRD 10 9 8 7 6 5 4 3 2 1

FOR MOM AND DAD

CONTENTS

ACKNOWLEDGMENTS

A couple of times each day, my resourceful daughter, Hannah, would break through one of her mother's various blockades and barge into my office, interruptions that made the laborious task of writing infinitely more tolerable. Thanks, Hannah. You truly are a blessing.

And, as always, I wish to thank my wife, Marlene, for her abiding support and love.

For research assistance, I wish to thank my friend and colleague, Lisa Vannais Shultz, as well as Mary Bishop and Adam Schmidt. Thanks also to Rand Jerris of the United States Golf Association and to former USGA presidents Frank Tatum and Grant Spaeth and former USGA executive director Frank Hannigan for their help.

Finally, my heartfelt appreciation to my editors at HarperCollins— Diane Reverand and Hugh Van Dusen—for their assistance and expertise, and to my agent, Freya Manston, for her enthusiastic support and indefatigable efforts on my behalf.

Playing in the U.S. Open is like tiptoeing through hell.
—*Professional golfer Jerry McGee*

INTRODUCTION

The symbol of U.S. Open futility, the ultimate Open victim, was Ray Ainsley, a player who left the golf world nothing by which to remember him other than one unfortunate skirmish he had with a hazard in the 1938 U.S. Open at Cherry Hills in Denver.

Ainsley required an Open-record nineteen strokes to complete the tenth hole there, many of his swings coming in staccato fashion in a hazard as the ball steadfastly refused to budge. Once Ainsley stopped thrashing, according to Open lore, a little girl was overheard saying, "Mommy, it must be dead now, because the man has stopped hitting it."

A little girl imagining that Ainsley was attempting to bludgeon some sort of creature may be apocryphal. It is nonetheless instructive, for the U.S. Open is a different kind of animal, one that does not acquiesce so effortlessly to professional golfers' manifest skills. The U.S. Open fights back.

The fact that it does so with such ferocity is the trait that sets the Open apart. It does so by design, of course, the United States Golf Association ensuring that the national championship is played on a course harder than college physics. P. J. Boatwright, then the executive director of the USGA and the man who approved the course setup that resulted in the Massacre at Winged Foot in 1974, shot an 84 at Winged Foot a few months before the Open. "I don't like to play Open courses," he said in a moment of candor.

No one else does, either. Sam Snead never won the U.S. Open and grew to loathe the tournament, the roots of his contempt taking hold early in his career, in only his third year on the Professional Golfers Association Tour. In 1939, the Open was played at Philadelphia Country Club, and Snead, twenty-seven at the time, needed only a bogey and par on the last two holes to win. He was unaware of what was required of him, however; there were no leaderboards in those days. Snead assumed he needed to birdie the final hole, causing him to take a more aggressive approach than was necessary. The upshot was that his aggressiveness malfunctioned and he took a triple-bogey 8 and finished fifth. "That night I was ready to go out with a gun and pay somebody to shoot me," he said.

Snead eventually came to understand the hold the Open has on golfers. It relentlessly tormented him, yet invariably he came back for more. "Everybody cusses the Open," he said once. "Then they can't wait to qualify the next year."

On one level, it is too appealing to dismiss offhandedly. The Open is one of the two or three most prestigious tournaments in the world; it is the national championship; and it truly is open, at least to those with a USGA Handicap Index that does not exceed 1.4. The club pro or the club champion cannot even begin to entertain thoughts that they might one day play in the Masters, an invitational tournament that requires that strict objectives be met before an invitation is tendered.

On another level, the Open has the power to humiliate and embarrass players as no other event can, and it exercises the power capriciously, without regard even to a player's historical significance, as Snead learned over a lifetime.

Each year, more than eight thousand golfers, pros and amateurs alike, pay their entry fee and attempt to qualify to play in the Open. Most are required to start with local qualifying, the survivors advancing to sectional qualifying. The reward for those who do qualify is also a risk. They will have the opportunity to play in the U.S. Open and might not break 80. Or even 90.

Tony Lopez was a sympathetic case in point, a qualifier playing at Pebble Beach in 1972. Lopez shot rounds of 86 and 91, a total of thirty-three-over par 177, numbers that failed to elude Los Angeles *Times* columnist Jim Murray, who never saw an overmatched golfer he was unwilling to belittle in print.

"You have to understand," Murray wrote, "the pros not only *volunteer* for this misery, but they *fight* to get in. Imagine a guy playing in two qualifying tournaments, then *paying* to play and then having a guy walking around behind you with a sign saying you're 33 over par. Tony Lopez ought to at least get Green Stamps."

Murray's writings frequently appear in these pages, for his words so often and so eloquently provided a fitting, clever, amusing summation of the Open about which he was writing. The U.S. Open was a hanging curveball for Murray, who time and again belted it out of the park. The man who once wrote from the Indianapolis 500, "Gentlemen, start your coffins," intuitively recognized that train wrecks were better copy than train rides, particularly, I would add, in his skilled fingers.

He wrote that "reporting the U.S. Open is like covering an execution. A circus fire. Bring a handkerchief." He wrote that "the U.S. Open is not a tournament, it's a hoodoo. . . . It's Hamlet with nine-irons. . . . A pox, not a play. . . . A movie where everybody dies in the end. . . . It is wicked, heartless, sardonic. . . . The Devil in cleats. . . . Beelzebub in plus fours. . . . A disaster masquerading as a game."

"Playing in the U.S. Open is not a privilege," Murray wrote from Oakland Hills in 1985, "it's a penance. But then you have to remember that people fought to get aboard the *Titanic,* too. And drew straws to get to go with Custer."

See, at the U.S. Open, the train wreck is built into the script. The difficulty of the course ensures it.

"The Open," Jack Nicklaus once said, "is seventy-two holes of bad breaks, with an occasional surprise."

It has always been that way, too. The surprise at the 1905 U.S. Open at the Myopia Hunt Club in South Hamilton, Massachusetts, was also a bad break. "Such a total lack of toilet appointments was never before witnessed at a championship event," *The Golfers' Magazine* wrote from the Myopia Hunt Club. Willie Anderson won there with a score of 314. Others can decide whether it was only a coincidence that this represented the highest winning Open score in the twentieth century.

"If you take it personally, you're in a lose-lose scenario," Canadian Richard Zokol said after completing the Open at Pebble Beach in 1992. "It's the U.S. Open. It's always unfair. Who said it's supposed to be fair? There's nothing wrong with going eighteen rounds with Godzilla."

Jim Murray, incidentally, would have loved Ray Ainsley, slugging away in the hazard as though he were a boxer with his opponent on the ropes. In reality, it was Ainsley who was on the ropes, as every U.S. Open competitor inevitably is. The best they can hope for is to fight from a clinch, to minimize the damage and hope that in the end the canvas is littered with the carcasses of their opponents, and that they are the last one standing, however precariously.

As for the little girl, she was wrong, of course. The man may have stopped hitting it, but it wasn't dead. Godzilla lives in perpetuity, returning each June under the banner of the United States Golf Association, under the guise of the United States Open.

TIPTOEING THROUGH HELL

1

BLUE BLAZERS AND DANDRUFF, LEATHER AND CHAINS

The golf gods to which the golfer occasionally refers, in the absence of a plausible explanation for the erratic behavior of his ball, largely have been misidentified. They are in fact the graybeards who run the United States Golf Association, power brokers eminently qualified, Lee Trevino once wryly observed, by virtue of their blue blazers and cans of dandruff. They wear authoritarian scowls, prescribed to them by their exalted status as arbiters of the rules of golf. They even wrote the book on the subject, cleverly entitled *The Rules of Golf*, an offering from the horror genre, as it were, its pages ascribing sinister penalties for venturing into foreboding hazards, its words void of compassion and demanding that we play the damn ball as it lies.

Yet, once a year they wield their power altruistically by exacting revenge on behalf of golfers at large, for whom ample greens and wide fairways still aren't of sufficient breadth to accommodate their slices and only stubbornly yield pars. For this faction of the golfing populace, the easiest courses in their community too often resemble the toughest courses in the country.

The game was designed to be difficult, yet week in and week out on the PGA Tour, professional golfers traipse across 7,200 yards of pitch-and-putt and shred the definition of par. Good for them, we say, but could they do so with our swings?

Each June, the USGA steps in and requires them to try, in a sense. It asks, with apologies to Bobby Jones, that they play a game with which we are more familiar, a game so confounding and difficult that in the midst of virtually every round we play we ponder trading in golf for a less disturbing hobby. Once a year, the USGA's blue blazers arrive to defend the game against its weekly assault by requiring that the best golfers in the world scramble to avoid triple-bogeys and to circumnavigate their way around a course that is as difficult for them as the local muny is for us.

They call this annual exercise the United States Open Championship.

The U.S. Open is one of the two or three most prestigious tournaments in the world, played on world-class courses that are not terribly forgiving of misguided shots under ordinary conditions. Then the USGA arrives, venom dripping, and transforms the course into a monster similar to that which Ben Hogan referred in describing Oakland Hills Country Club in Birmingham, Michigan, in the aftermath of his victory in the U.S. Open there in 1951.

This was the year that unofficially launched the era of the Open setup, the intentional process by the USGA of tweaking a course to give it the means necessary to defend itself against assaults on par. Typically, the USGA pinches the fairways until they scream. It allows the rough to grow untended, in the manner of a yard ignored while tenants are away on vacation. It denudes the greens, then deprives them of water to give them the consistency of asphalt.

"If the USGA could put lakes in the middle of every green they would," Dave Stockton once said, which may have been as much a statement of fact as it was his own frustration from failed attempts at Open survival.

The upshot is that playing a U.S. Open course is akin to walking blindly through a minefield, a single misstep capable of detonating a round and sending a score soaring. The errant tee shot likely will settle into rough so thick that only a sand wedge is capable of extricating it. The putt struck with even a hint of too much force gathers speed as it scoots past its target—where it will stop nobody knows.

Historians have argued that the U.S. Open is the USGA's annual censure of professional golf. Receiving remuneration for playing, in the opinion of the elitists who founded the USGA, debauches their game. When the USGA began conducting its national championships, the Open was an afterthought; the inaugural U.S. Open was played the day after the inaugural U.S. Amateur in 1895.

The aristocracy for whom the game ostensibly was invented viewed the golf professional as it would another manservant. Indeed, until the flamboyant pro Walter Hagen brazenly entered the clubhouse uninvited, in effect opening its doors in perpetuity on behalf of his brethren, the professional golfer was a second-class citizen who hung his hat from a nail in a country club backroom.

The USGA, moreover, has always been the governing body of *amateur* golf in America, inherently implying a disdain for those paid to play. Their penance for debasing the game is the U.S. Open, a tournament which extracts a mental and physical toll to a degree that its contestants rue the day they chose to make a career of golf.

To win the Open, you do so by default, the trophy going to the last man standing. "Nobody wins the Open," former PGA Tour player Dr. Cary Middlecoff said. "It wins you." Supporting testimony comes from the fact that until Payne Stewart holed a fifteen-foot putt at the seventy-second and last hole to win the U.S. Open at Pinehurst in 1999 no one had ever won the Open by making a putt of any considerable length at the final hole. As it was, Stewart's putt was for par, which he needed to hole to protect his one-stroke lead. The final-hole birdie to win an Open remains an abstract concept; birdies are scarce on an Open course, but Open pressure has hunted them nearly to extinction by late Sunday afternoon.

Professional golfers view these exceedingly difficult courses with the same disdain they would have for, say, a courtesy car with an empty gas tank. When they encounter an Open setup, they routinely cry foul, usually as a means by which they can anesthetize a severely bruised ego. One player, Clayton Heafner, was said to have so detested the Open and its narrow fairways and thick rough that he dreamed of having a one-foot putt to win, so that he could amble up to the ball and casually backhand it off the green and into the crowd as he uttered, "Fuck it," for all to hear, notably the USGA.

"The Open," Art Wall once said, decrying the obstacles to scoring well that the USGA created, "is the World Series of golf, and the baseball people don't put rocks in the infield at the World Series."

This is true only in the literal sense. There are, indeed, obstacles to winning the World Series, notably a quality opponent. Put a defenseless opponent in the field and a team is certain to put up an impressive score, similar to the way a defenseless course allows golfers to routinely post low scores. The New York Yankees represent the rocks in the infield.

The U.S. Open is supposed to be difficult to win. "If it isn't the premier championship in the world," said Sandy Tatum, a former USGA president and among the most influential men in the game, "then it's one of them. We're dealing with the world's best players, in one of the world's best championships, and we have to give them a golf course that will, A, challenge them, and, B, separate the wheat from the chaff. We want to make them hit the ball into the fairway, and if they don't, they have to pay a price for it. We want to make them hit the ball on the green, and if they don't they have to pay another price.

And it also matters where you put the ball on the green in relation to the hole."

The inherent problem is that professional golfers unanimously consider themselves the wheat and are horrified to discover that on more difficult golf courses, they are more likely to fulfill the role of chaff. Those accustomed to breaking 70 are not particularly fond of layouts on which breaking 80 is rarely a given.

"Professionals complain a lot, I've found," wrote course architect Robert Trent Jones in his book, *Golf's Magnificent Challenge*. "They seem to want fairway traps from which they can reach the green, holes that are not too long, rough that is not too deep, greens that are dead-flat. That may be an exaggeration, but they do seem to object to severe tests. Perhaps if I made my living playing golf, I would feel the same, but the fact is that if we turn golf into a putting contest nobody will care and there won't be a living."

Golfers of every ilk love courses on which they have played well and decry those on which their self-esteem is demolished. "The quality of a golf course is usually in the eye of the beholder," Jones wrote. "Usually the view depends on the beholder's success that day." A contemporary case in point: In the midst of a year in which he played the best golf of his career, Kirk Triplett shot 84 and 77 on the weekend of the 2000 Open at Pebble Beach, then indicated sadism was at the root of the USGA's machinations. "I hate to see the old girl in leather and chains, which is what the USGA put her in," a disconsolate Triplett said.

The PGA Tour's constituency vociferously argues that fans prefer to see birdies to bogeys, though its point is arguable. If the public was ravenous in its desire to witness flocks of birds, crowds at Senior PGA Tour events would not be so sparse. For the seniors, fairways historically have been generous, the rough nonpenal, and pins placed on greens in positions which the majority of the field can locate without topography charts. The courses have been relatively easy, birdies abundant, and eyewitnesses scarce.

The late sports columnist Jim Murray might have been writing on *behalf* of the masses rather than *for* them, when in his autobiography, he wrote, "I have a confession to make. When it comes to tournament golf, I root for the course. In rodeos, I root for the bulls. And the broncs. In golf, I root for the real estate. I'm a big fan of double bogeys. I love it when the weather at Pebble Beach is blowing a force ten gale and the flags are bent horizontal in the wind. I love unputtable greens."

Murray surely viewed Sunday at the Open at Pebble Beach in 1992 as among the great days in sports history. The greens were so parched that they had begun to turn brown. The wind blew hard off Carmel Bay, bending pins and whipping flags and wreaking havoc with skills incapable of withstanding intemperate weather when it and a typical U.S. Open setup have conspired against them.

Weekend players can relate, which contributes to the appeal the Open holds for the masses. From their vantage point—standing over their ball on the first tee, preparing to lash at it with a swing ill suited to execute the task—even the easiest courses often play as though the USGA had prepared them for the Open. "If there's one thing that discourages me about the game of golf," Murray once wrote, "it's to see a pro shoot a 62 from the back tees of a course I can't break 100 on."

Of course, the courses on which Murray was incapable of breaking 100 may have included all of them, but that would be missing his point. The truth is that Murray enjoyed seeing the best players in the world occasionally challenged to a degree that he was with every shot. Indeed, he once wrote that he was "a tremendous fan of triple bogeys."

His view was supported by an unscientific Internet poll conducted by *Sports Illustrated* in 2000, asking the question: Which do you prefer, Tour events that are birdie-fests, like the Hope, or tournaments in which par is a good score, like the U.S. Open? Ninety-two percent of nearly 5,500 responses cited pars, 8 percent birdies.

It is not a theory that has evolved, but one that has endured. When the 1963 U.S. Open was won with a score of nine-over par,

Arthur Daley wrote in *The New York Times*: "Every hacker in America had to rub his hands in unholy glee at such mass discomfiture."

"I think a lot of it has to do with numbers," said Frank Hannigan, a former executive director of the USGA and an ABC golf analyst. "On a typical PGA Tour setup, you only have two kinds of scores, pars or birdies. In an Open, big scores loom. I think the uncertainty is a lot more fun than just birdies and pars."

The uncertainty often evolves from leather and chains, which command as prominent a place in the USGA's closet as blue blazers and dandruff cans. Yet a case could be made that, even presented provocatively, Pebble Beach had never looked better than it did for the Open that year. The condition of the course was immaculate, a word seldom associated with a heavily played course open to the public. If Tiger Woods had been judging a beauty contest in which Pebble Beach was entered as it was presented for the 2000 Open, he'd be crowning it the queen. To Woods, who put 15 strokes between him and the rest of the field, Pebble Beach represented a work of art. One man's dominatrix is another man's Mona Lisa.

By its very nature, golf is unfair. As a hedge against its inherent inequity which drives golfers crazy, *the rub of the green* became part of the lexicon of golf, a simple term on which an unseemly and inexplicable turn of fortune can be blamed.

Once a year, the USGA co-opts the rub of the green, requiring a U.S. Open field of 156 players to have to deal with it for eighteen tortuous holes. It once did so in part by steadfastly declining to adhere to its own guidelines set forth in *The Rules of Golf*, Appendix IV, *Miscellaneous*, "Par Computation." "Par," the rule read, "is the score that an expert golfer would be expected to make for a given hole. Par means errorless play without flukes and under ordinary weather conditions, allowing two strokes on the putting green."

Presumably, those competing in the U.S. Open qualify as expert golfers, yet few ever complete 72 holes in even par. When Tiger Woods won the 2000 Open at Pebble Beach, he was twelve-under par, a record score that was not indicative of the USGA's failure to sharpen Pebble's teeth. It was instead a testament to Woods's skill. Ernie Els and Miguel Angel Jiminez tied for second, 15 strokes in arrears, at three-*over* par, a number more representative of the course's difficulty quotient.

The USGA now routinely ignores what until 2000 were its guidelines in establishing par on certain holes. Its rules used to say that any hole 471 yards or longer should be a par 5, and that "yardages for guidance in computing par . . . should not be applied arbitrarily."

The second hole at Pebble Beach has always been a par 5 of more than 500 yards, as it was for the U.S. Open played there in 1972, 1982, and 1992. For the 2000 Open, the USGA arbitrarily decreed that it would be played as a par 4, even at 484 yards. It noted the untimely demise of a pair of Monterey pine trees that once ominously framed the green, threatening to slap down second shots lacking precision. Without them, the USGA was saying, 4 was "the score that an expert golfer would be expected to make."

The statistics for the week revealed that the hole ought to have been played as a par 4.5. The average score was 4.42, nearly a half stroke over par, rendering it the fourth toughest hole on the course.

The USGA steadfastly insists that scores are immaterial, that it matters not whether the winning number is six over or six under. Yet it would require a skilled attorney's deftness at manipulating the truth to provide a convincing argument on the USGA's behalf.

Midway through the 2000 Open at Pebble, the USGA chose not to water already parched greens, and when the trademark winds came up on Saturday, the third round became a survival test. The scoring average for the sixty-three players who made the cut was 77.12. "I think they [the USGA officials] are so worried that the scores are going to be good that they let it get away from them," John Huston said.

The USGA routinely transforms par 5s into par 4s; it is among its defense mechanisms against low scoring against par. Courses that typically play to a par of 72 will be trimmed to a par of 71 or even into a par of 70. The members, for instance, play the Olympic Club in Daly City, California, as a par 72. The Open there played to a par 71. The USGA trims two strokes from par at Oakland Hills, reducing it from 72 to 70, by transforming a pair of par 5s into par 4s.

"All you have to do is take one hole that's called a par 5 and don't do anything to it and call it a par 4," Frank Hannigan said. "It's a mind game."

Jack Nicklaus, whose history at Pebble Beach is unparalleled, railed against the USGA's decision to turn the second hole into a par 4, suggesting that it ought to have remained a par 5 for the sake of historical comparison. Of course, had it been played as a par 5, Woods's winning score would have been sixteen-under par, a number by which the USGA would have been embarrassed, even coming from the best player in history.

A more sinister mechanism is simply to alter the playing characteristics of a hole. The only U.S. Open Arnold Palmer ever won was in 1960 at Cherry Hills in Denver, and he did so by shooting a final-round 65 that began when he drove the green on the 346-yard par-4 first hole, a dramatic start to a memorable finish. From the USGA's perspective, this was unacceptable behavior, even from a budding icon. When the Open returned to Cherry Hills in 1978, the hole measured 399 yards, rendering the green impossible to reach with a single shot.

The USGA does not always wait that long to correct what it deems a flaw. In 1979, the Open went to Inverness Club in Toledo, which had undergone a partial redesign for the Open. The new par-5 eighth hole had a severe dogleg left. When Lon Hinkle arrived at the eighth tee in the first round, he took note of a gap in the trees to the left of the tee box, leading to an adjacent fairway, the seventeenth, from which the eighth green was reasonably accessible, more so surely than it was from the middle of the proper fairway. Hinkle took a one-iron, and hit it through the gap and onto the seventeenth fairway, dramatically reducing the yardage of the hole. He was left with a three-iron second to the eighth green, then took two putts for an easy birdie.

Overnight, a twenty-four-foot Black Hills spruce tree had sprung from the ground in a strategic place, plugging much of the gap through which Hinkle's tee shot had traveled. The USGA in fact had planted it at five o'clock on the morning of the second round to discourage players from attempting similar derring-do from the tee box. It became known as the Hinkle Tree.

This represented a rare instance when the USGA called an audible. Ordinarily, it does not stray from its game plan, culled from a formula designed to exact its revenge and to prevent the chaos that reined in the '55 Open at the Olympic Club, where the rough was so debilitating that for those hitting their tee shot into it, it was akin to a one-shot penalty, the same as it would be for hitting into a lateral water hazard.

The authors of the course-setup protocol were Joe Dey, the USGA executive director at the time, and USGA president Richard Tufts, whose family owned the acclaimed Pinehurst resort in North Carolina. "Tufts and Dey called for rough that would be the equivalent of a half-stroke penalty," Hannigan wrote for *Golf Digest*, "one that would allow the player to advance the ball purposefully but without being able to stop it on the greens." The intermediate rough, or first cut (or semi-rough, as it was called in Britain) is cut to two inches. Next was the primary rough, grown to five or six inches, and with modern agronomy practices, is usually consistent and thick as well. The fairways typically are thirty to forty yards wide, depending on the lengths of holes.

"In the Open, every tee shot matters a lot," Hannigan said.

The USGA even employs a Cost of Rough Index to measure its success in achieving a half-stroke penalty for missing the fairway. The Index was developed by Hannigan and Dean Knuth, the USGA's senior director of handicapping in the 1980s and most of the '90s. On the fourteen non-par-3 holes, it compares scores made from the fairway to those made outside the fairway. When the average difference is around a half stroke, the USGA has accomplished its goal.

A device known as a Stimpmeter is used to measure the speed of greens. Designed by Edward S. Stimpson in 1936, this device is a simple ramp placed at an angle of forty-five degrees to a flat green. A ball is released at the top of the ramp, and the distance it rolls, once it reaches the putting surface, is the Stimp reading for the green. The USGA began using a Stimpmeter to measure Open greens in 1978 and typically aims for a reading of eleven (for eleven feet), which is not altogether unlike putting on a pane of glass. On relatively flat greens on which typically it would be easier to putt, it attempts to achieve a reading of twelve or higher.

"The greens," Hannigan wrote, "starved and on a life-support system for the week, will never reveal a ball mark. In Stimpmeter terms, they are an honest eleven."

The result is a golf course on which the layman—an amateur with handicaps of ten or higher—cannot be expected to have a great deal of fun. The USGA says that those with handicaps of ten should be expected to shoot 91 on an Open course and an Open setup. Hannigan places the number at 100, by factoring in the debilitating mental toll taken in the course of a five-hour round in which even the simplest of strokes—the two-foot putt—is potentially hazardous.

The most obvious indicator that the USGA indeed does care about scores occurred in 1974, a year after Johnny Miller had the audacity to win the Open at Oakmont by shooting a final-round 63, an affront to the USGA. A 63 wins the Bob Hope Chrysler Classic, not the United States Open. When the cries of sacrilege subsided, the USGA ostensibly redoubled its efforts to ensure that no such ignominy would be committed in the future. The result was the infamous Massacre at Winged Foot in 1974, won by Hale Irwin with a score of seven-over par.

It was in the midst of the massacre that Tatum, a high-ranking member of the USGA executive committee (and then a future president of the USGA), attempted a spirited defense of the course and its setup and issued a quote that, once the media had buffed and polished it over the years, became the organization's unofficial mission statement on Open setups.

"Our intention," Tatum said, more or less, "is not to embarrass the greatest players in the world, but to identify them."

The words receive an annual press recitation once the complaints begin anew about the difficulty of the course on which the Open is being played. Critics often accuse the USGA of failing on this count, citing players with similar skills who have won the U.S. Open but no other major championships, including Tom Kite and Corey Pavin, each of whom won the Open once, two-time winners Lee Janzen and Curtis Strange, and Hale Irwin, a three-time winner. None were considered long hitters, yet each of them was exceedingly accurate.

This often invites criticism that Open layouts favor particular-type players, the short, straight hitters, while generally eliminating the longer drivers, who tend toward wildness.

"It can't be everything to everybody," Hannigan said. "What the setups do essentially is to maximize the accuracy part of the game, particularly about hitting the ball in the fairway and hitting the ball on the green. There are parts of the game that suffer. It doesn't matter as much how far you hit it, and you can't have the display of artistry, as people call it, around the greens."

Among those who never won an Open were Sam Snead and, not surprisingly, the Spaniard Seve Ballesteros, who won five other major championships, including two Masters. Ballesteros was a brilliant player, whose short-game magic and ability to manufacture creative shots from the woods and other dubious places diminished the damage his erratic driving otherwise might have caused. Wild tee shots did not abjectly penalize him at Augusta National, which features wide fairways and virtually no rough.

Ballesteros took his typically erratic game to the Open, where the deep rough stifles creative recoveries, in effect paralyzing his ability to play well. When Lee Trevino congratulated Ballesteros on winning the Masters in 1980 and reminded him that he was responsible for suggesting that he go to Augusta a week early to practice, Ballesteros sought additional advice.

"How," he asked Trevino, "do I win the U.S. Open?"

"Get them to cut down the rough," Trevino replied lightly, but frankly.

Narrow Open fairways haunted Ballesteros, to the extent that each year they seemed to close in on him more and more. Ballesteros mused that eventually an Open course might feature only rough and green, at which point he might have a chance to win.

Ballesteros has admitted a disdain for the U.S. Open. "Sure, it's a major," he said, "but it's not a good tournament because eighty percent of the game in the U.S. Open is about hitting the fairways. It takes away the skill factor. Everyone wants to compete in the U.S. Open, but then when they get there they all hope the week would end quickly."

Indeed, only the winner walks away, having concluded the experience was fun. The sense one gets from observing the USGA over the years is that the hallmark of the U.S. Open should be a winning score over par. No doubt it rankles the hierarchy that it no longer seems capable of achieving this goal. Not since 1978 has an Open been won with a score over par, though the winning number typically is reasonably close to even par.

This assault on par on historic venues was at the core of the stand the USGA elected to make in 1998 against technological advances in equipment. "It's fairly obvious today that there is a burgeoning number of superb athletes playing the game," USGA President F. Morgan Taylor said in his inaugural address in January of 1998. "That it's likely to increase is also fairly obvious, what with the Tiger Woods phenomenon and purses of $3 million every week just around the corner. These superb athletes have better equipment, perfectly tuned to their requirements for maximum efficiency. They play on new grasses which can be conditioned for consistently fast surfaces. Sufficient varieties of golf balls are available to the great players, allowing them to select the one that provides aerodynamic qualities exactly suited to their swings. These facts and others such as strenuous on-site physical training have combined to threaten the obsolescence for many of golf's historic venues."

Among them is the East Course at Merion Golf Club in Ardmore, Pennsylvania, host of five U.S. Opens, including those won by Bobby Jones in 1930 and Ben Hogan in 1950. At 6,544 yards, the course is deemed too short to accommodate the modern players' power games and as a result is no longer an adequate Open test.

This was the gauntlet, defiantly thrown at the manufacturers who were nearly unanimously in favor of the status quo: no restrictions on technological advances in equipment. A few months after his inaugural address, Taylor emphatically reiterated his position in an interview with *Golf World* magazine. "Our franchise," he said, "is to preserve and protect the game's ancient and honorable traditions. I intend to do that, and there's not one lawyer in the world who is going to get in our way of doing that."

A year later, the USGA put into place a test for springlike effect in thin-faced metal woods, establishing a limit on the rebound capacity of a ball and, in effect, drawing a line on a driver's contribution to the distance a ball is hit. The equipment industry predictably cried foul, but the USGA in fact was simply taking a page from its past.

Nearly half a century earlier, the USGA was concerned that stronger, better players were capitalizing on modern technology, loosely identified then by wound golf balls and steel shafts that had rendered wooden shafts obsolete. It chose to counter by agreeing to have course architect Robert Trent Jones make over Oakland Hills, host of the 1951 U.S. Open, by providing the course with the tools necessary to defend itself. "The purpose," Jones wrote, "was to restore the playing values that had been lost because of advances in technology and the abilities of accomplished golfers."

Jones created a brutal test, and, in the process, ushered in the era of the Open course setup that fifty years later continues to confound the game's best players in their perennial quest to tiptoe through hell without getting scorched.

"I wish we had to play these courses every week," Mike Reid once said. "We'd all be better players. Of course, I might be brain-damaged."

Kenny Lee Puckett, the protagonist in the Dan Jenkins novel *Dead Solid Perfect*, may have had it just right when it occurred to him that he might be in over his head in the midst of the first round of a fictional Open on a fictional and onerous course. "Oh, Lord," Kenny Lee said, "I don't want the cheese, I just want out of the trap."

2

THE MONSTER

The pigeon perch adjacent to the putting green at the Riviera Country Club in Pacific Palisades, California, bears only a passing resemblance to Ben Hogan, betraying the sculptor's efforts at replicating the great man in stone. Moreover, the artist egregiously erred in cropping Hogan's club, creating the image, as more than one observer has noted, that Hogan is gripping something more personal than his driver.

An even greater indignity was that the statue deprived Hogan of the stature he had earned at Riviera. The sculptor's chisel cut him off at the knees, in effect accomplishing what the United States Golf Association failed to do in 1948, when the club hosted the U.S. Open.

Herein lie the roots of the USGA's mean streak as it pertains to its showcase event.

These roots run deep in the soil at Riviera, perennial site of the

Nissan (nee Los Angeles) Open. Riviera is blanketed in kikuyu, a weedlike grass with a sturdy root structure that deters eradication. When kikuyu rough is permitted to grow unabated, the result is an ornery, wiry Velcro-like surface from which it is difficult to advance the ball with any authority or direction.

Kikuyu, however, is virtually dormant in the winter, when the PGA Tour makes its annual visit to Riviera. So when Ben Hogan won the Los Angeles Open with a score of nine-under par 275 there in 1948, he was not fooled by its temperate nature, and cautioned against expecting similar scores when the players returned to Riviera for the U.S. Open that summer.

"Let me warn you not to be misled by my nine-under-par total," Hogan said. "The course is certain to play 6 to 8 strokes harder in the Open. Personally, I think a score of 282 to 284 will win the Open in June."

These kinds of numbers would have been acceptable to Joseph C. Dey, the executive director of the USGA and a man who saw the U.S. Open not as a tournament so much as a torture chamber, a survival-of-the-fittest exercise. "Joe," long-time Riviera member Jim Murray wrote in the introduction to Geoff Shackelford's book, *The Riviera Country Club: A Definitive History*, "was always afraid someone would shoot 60 in an Open and he'd have to jump off a building."

Taking note of Hogan's score of 275 in the Los Angeles Open, Dey decreed that Riviera was too passive. He requested that the club allow its trademark kikuyu grass to grow to six inches in height in the rough, a debilitating altitude, given kikuyu's rancorous disposition at any height other than that employed in its fairways. Willie Hunter, the club's resident pro, was an accomplished player, a former British Amateur champion who understood the game's elemental challenges and how they would expand exponentially, were the kikuyu rough permitted to grow unchecked. Hunter informed Dey that were he to prevail in his request, "No one will break 300."

A score of 300 or higher had not won the Open since Tommy Armour's victory at Oakmont Country Club in 1927. Still, the prospect of the Open champion winning with a score of 300 must have been a tantalizing one to Dey.

Host clubs in those days had greater leverage in the setup of the course than they do now, when the USGA's recommendations are expected to be followed and it dispatches its own staff to monitor preparations months in advance. Back then, the host club took recommendations under advisement and arrived at its own decision. Dey deferred to Hunter, a decision he rationalized by noting that the length of the course (7,020 yards, the longest in Open history to that point) in all likelihood would ensure an adequate difficulty quotient.

Hunter and his staff chose to keep the rough at a manageable height of three inches. Hogan again was victorious, this time winning with a score of 276, only a stroke worse than his Los Angeles Open score. Moreover, Hogan eclipsed the U.S. Open record by five strokes, a performance that ought to have been applauded and left at that. "Hogan would have broken the record if they played the Open on an ice floe that year," Murray wrote. Instead, Dey looked beyond Hogan's immeasurable skill as well as his command of Riviera (which eventually came to be known as Hogan's Alley), and noted that Jimmy Demaret and Jim Turnesa also bettered the previous Open record. This served as a distress signal to Dey, who concluded that he had not aggressively enough defended his instinct to heighten the rough and that the Open had paid a price that he deemed unacceptable.

Dey did not jump off a bridge, perhaps to the chagrin of generations of players who ultimately have had to pay a penance for Riviera's benevolence. Instead, he vowed that no course under his watch would venture into war without a full complement of weapons to adequately defend itself.

The dye was cast. The following two Opens were each won with scores over par—gratifyingly, surely, from the USGA's perspective—

but the USGA had set its sights on the 1951 Open scheduled to be played on the South Course at Oakland Hills Country Club in Birmingham, Michigan, outside Detroit.

Oakland Hills had been built in 1918 and was designed by Donald Ross, a renowned architect who delivered a course that by the standards of the day was among the most difficult in golf. When the Open was first played there in 1924, Cyril Walker won with a score of nine-over par.

The Open's return engagement in 1937 sounded an alarm. By then, steel had begun to replace hickory in shafts, the balls were better, and technology was simplifying the game. Ralph Guldahl won the '37 Open with an Open-record score of seven-under par, sixteen strokes better than Walker's winning score thirteen years earlier.

The chairman of the greens committee at Oakland Hills was John Oswald, an engineer at Ford Motor Company and a headstrong man known as Big John. It was said of Big John that he favored a greens committee with an odd number of members and that three was too many. Oswald and his committee of one decided that Oakland Hills was in dire need of a face-lift and that it should be performed with the intention of allowing the course to put its best face forward in the 1951 U.S. Open. He was of the mind that the star of the U.S. Open should be the golf course, particularly his own. "The Open is the greatest title there is," Oswald said. "The course should be so hard, nobody can win it."

These words represented a sonata to Dey and the USGA. By then, the USGA was concerned that unless it began taking appropriate measures, the historic layouts on which it held its championships would be insufficiently difficult and ultimately obsolete, an unacceptable outcome.

Oswald and Dey were kindred spirits who agreed that in the absence of Donald Ross (who had died in 1948) Robert Trent Jones was the man on whom they would call to perform the requisite reconstructive surgery on Oakland Hills. In the aftermath of the 1948 Open at Riviera, Jones was hired by Oakland Hills, with the consent of the USGA, which for the first time deliberately set out to concoct a course that was certain to upstage the players.

Jones, a Cornell graduate, was already a preeminent course architect, one who by virtue of his work at Oakland Hills and subsequent Open projects became known as the Open doctor. He was a proud, stubborn man who assiduously defended his work, even against assaults from prominent tour professionals. In later years, he would routinely trade barbs with Jack Nicklaus, who largely despised Jones's work and never bothered to veil the fact ("Excuse me, while I go throw up," he once said when asked for his opinion of Hazeltine Golf Club, a Jones design and an Open course).

Jones's defiance was legendary. At another Open course on which he worked—the Lower Course at Baltusrol Golf Club in Springfield, New Jersey—a member of the club once complained to Jones that the remodeled par-3 fourth hole, 194-yards over water, was too difficult. Jones escorted the member, along with the club pro Johnny Farrell and tournament chairman C. P. Burgess, to the fourth tee box to test the hole. After the other three men each hit their ball onto the green, Jones pulled a mashie (a mid-iron) from his bag, put down a ball, and struck it. The ball alighted on the green, took a single bounce, and vanished into the cup, a hole-in-one.

"Gentlemen," Jones said as he turned to his astonished onlookers, never skipping a beat, "I think the hole is eminently fair." Jones later mused that it was the most renowned shot ever hit outside of tournament play.

Jones's assignment at Oakland Hills, to deliver a course on which even the best players in the world would be uncomfortable, made him a visible target for those with or without enough game to meet his challenge. True to his nature, he pressed on unfettered, determined to produce a course capable of repelling lesser players who "crash their way around easy layouts, posting scores that make them appear like great players, when actually lacking the finesse to be front-ranking performers."

In the process, he redefined course architecture, requiring that tee shots be directed toward a landing area rather than the more receptive, generous fairway, and that approach shots be directed toward targets on greens, rather than toward greens themselves. "In a nutshell," Jones wrote in the June 1951 issue of *Golfing* magazine, "Oakland Hills has been redesigned with target areas to be hit from the tee [and by second shots on the long holes] and with pin areas to be aimed for at the green." In either case, Jones had substantially reduced the size of the goal. His objective, he said, was "to give the pros the shock treatment." He set a winning score of 286 or higher as the test to determine whether he had accomplished his objective.

Among Jones's first tasks was to commission a study on tour players' driving distances. He learned that the average drive traveled 236 yards in the air, while a handful of players were capable of routinely hitting it 250 yards in the air. He, too, noted that in 1924, driving contests were won with shots no more than 260 yards, while in 1951, winning drives measured up to 300 yards. He read in the July 1924 issue of *Golf Illustrated* that at Oakland Hills "the par 4 holes are of such length that only the longer players are able to reach in two, and they must hit drivers nearly always of two hundred fifty yards, and follow them with full brassies [three-woods]."

Jones knew that, were Oakland Hills to be left alone, the players in 1951 would be hitting drivers and mid- to short-irons into the greens on the par 4s. "A great golf course," he concluded, "lay virtually defenseless."

"With the ball and equipment having progressed so far," Jones wrote in USGA *Journal and Turf Management*, "is it not only fair to assume that the architecture of Oakland Hills had to be brought up to a standard comparable to the shot requirements asked of the players during the Open Championship of 1924? I, for one, cannot concede that the current golfers are more powerful than the greats of former years. Gene Sarazen at fifty-one is hitting the ball twenty-five to thirty-five yards farther than he did during the Open Championship of 1924."

Donald Ross's original fairway bunkers at Oakland Hills now came up short of the landing area, rendering them irrelevant. Jones countered by filling them in and constructing new tiers of fairway bunkers, from 230 to 270 yards from the tee, in an effort to have them catch either a short hitter's tee shot or a long hitter's tee ball. "He wanted the penalty for a bad drive to be the same for a Sam Snead, who drove it in the third bunker, as it was for Jerry Barber, who hit it in the first one," Jones's son, Rees, also a course architect and the reigning Open doctor, told *Sports Illustrated*.

Jones was meticulous in his effort to ensure that his bunkers were equal-opportunity antagonists. One story had Ben Hogan on the practice green there in the midst of the Oakland Hills makeover, when Jones asked him what he thought of the new fairway bunkers on the tenth hole. "Too close," Hogan was said to have replied. Jones was bewildered by the response. To prove his point to Jones, Hogan pulled out his driver and teed up a ball adjacent to the practice green, then crushed a drive that cleared the distant bunkers. A short time later, Jones had installed another bunker where Hogan's tee shot landed.

Jones's handiwork, which resulted in sixty-six new bunkers replacing obsolete ones, was not going unnoticed. A full seven months before the Open was to be played, Marshall Dunn wrote in the *Detroit Free-Press*, "Winter snows are about to hide some fearful things which are taking place at Oakland Hills Country Club."

The alarm sounded by Dunn resonated as far as away as Far Hills, New Jersey, home of the USGA. Its hierarchy became concerned that Jones was venturing beyond the bounds of fair play, even as he had been given wide latitude. The USGA demanded that the reconstruction be stopped pending an investigation. Eventually, the USGA concluded that Jones had not abandoned his blueprint and work resumed.

In the meantime, the USGA sought to allay growing concern that the course had been made too tough. In the spring of 1951, several prominent players made their way to Detroit to inspect Jones's work and to provide their stamps of approval. Among them was Gene

Sarazen, who called it "the greatest test of golf I've seen in a long time." Byron Nelson gave it his blessing, as well.

Only Sam Snead failed to follow the script. Following a practice round in which he shot a three-over par 73, he called Oakland Hills, "a nightmare. Awful. We've got to play it, but we don't have to like it."

Snead later elaborated, "You can't play short, you can't play safe, and you can't play bold. If you're short, you have long irons left on your second shots and if you hit them to the greens they won't hold."

The USGA chose to contribute to the players' misery by framing the course in fescue rough that in some places pinched the landing areas to a width of only nineteen yards, in the process, replicating an hourglass figure that was not in the least seductive to this group of men. "You have to walk down these fairways single file," Dr. Cary Middlecoff said. Herb Graffis wrote in *Golfing* magazine that the bunkers squeezed the fairways "like sinister Don Juans on the make."

Once again, the USGA ignored its own guidelines regarding course setups for its events. "It is desired to require greater accuracy from the tees by making all rough deeper and by narrowing the fairways between two-hundred-forty and three-hundred yards," the *USGA Golf Championship Manual* read. "The narrowing should be gradual, commencing perhaps at two-hundred-thirty yards and reaching the narrowest part of from thirty-five to forty yards at about two hundred eighty yards from the tee."

The rough was said to have been so tall that it collapsed under its own weight. "I remember walking down the seventh fairway and the fescue was knee-high," said Peter Jackson, once an Oakland Hills member whose family owned a home near the third green there. "I found seventeen balls in that stuff." Dan Jenkins called it "the kind of course where you could lose your feet."

Willard Mullin, the renowned sports cartoonist for the *New York World Telegram*, depicted Oakland Hills as "The Monster," providing an enduring and defining moniker. Golf writers ascribed variations on the theme, including the Green Monster, Frankenstein, and Oakland Ogre.

Even by shortening the course, Jones toughened it. He took 110 yards from its distance, much of it the result of having cropped a pair of short par 5s and turning them into long 4s that played 458 and 459 yards. This was straight from the Jones primer on golf course design; he believed in holes that stubbornly relinquished pars, but generously dispensed bogeys. Given the elementary understanding that achieving par is more difficult on a long 4 than a short 5, Jones had vastly increased the potential for bogey by reducing par from 72 to 70.

The greens at Oakland Hills were already treacherous, a fact duly noted by Jones. "If Oakland Hills put their pins as close to the edge of the greens as they do at Augusta," he said, "nobody would break par." They were defenseless only in front. Donald Ross, the original designer, had left them unguarded, to accommodate the bump-and-run shots that players in earlier eras were required to hit in the absence of equipment capable of hitting high, spinning shots that landed softly and held greens. Jones countered with steep bunkers designed to penalize those shots hit short, reducing the margin for error.

"The truly great and accurate shots will earn their just rewards," he said. "The slightest miss or badly executed shot will be punished. A great champion should emerge."

Jones's malevolence made him at least as unpopular as a snap hook, maybe more so, given the fact that the snap hook usually visits unexpectedly and only occasionally. Jones's holes were there to stay, eighteen a day confronting the players, for four days. "If I had to play this course for a living every week, I'd get into another business," Hogan said. In a practice round, Hogan flew the eighteenth green with a long iron. "No one can play some of these holes," he said to his caddie. He predicted a winning score near 290.

Hogan's course management was ordinarily exemplary, but even he struggled to concoct a sound game plan. The course, he said, favored the player who was unusually short from the tee, but unusually long with his irons, a player who did not exist, given the contradictory parameters Hogan cited. The safe play was to lay up short of the fairway bunkers, to avoid their penal nature. Doing so, however, left the player with a long iron or fairway wood to the green, an antidote to low scoring.

Even Jones understood the inherent drawback to such a strategy. Those in contention, he said, would be "the boys who are not underclubbing. Anyone playing safe is at too much of a disadvantage fighting the chips and putts on these green contours. And if they are in the rough, it's much better to be closer to the pin."

Still, Hogan decided that accurate long-iron shots were critical to playing well at Oakland Hills, and he spent the better part of a day on the practice tee hitting three-irons.

Perhaps he hit his long irons too well, for in the opening round, Hogan frequently hit approach shots over the green. He needed 76 strokes, including 6 at the par-4 eighteenth, to complete the first round, leaving him 5 shots in arrears of the leader, Sam Snead.

He fared marginally better in the second round, shooting a 73 that still left him trailing fifteen other players, including the leader, Bobby Locke, by the same five-stroke deficit he faced after round one.

"It was nice to see the golfers placing their shots for a change," said the legend Walter Hagen, Oakland Hills's first professional. "The man who wins here will be the player who knows what he can do, and tries to do it."

Hogan's task was daunting; in those days, the final two rounds of the Open were played on the same day, on Saturday, and any notion that a player could erase a significant margin was tempered by the fact that through thirty-six holes, not a single player had played a round under par and only two, Dave Douglas and Johnny Bulla, had played a round in even-par 70. The great Sam Snead, the first-round leader, shot a 78 in the second round.

"I'd have to be Houdini to win now," Hogan said. "I need one-forty and how can anybody shoot one-forty on this course?"

Two years earlier, Hogan had nearly lost his life in an automobile accident and had suffered extensive damage to his legs. After the second round, he repaired to his room and spent much of the evening soaking his legs in a hot tub, meanwhile pondering how to free himself from the shackles Jones had built into the course. Ultimately, he decided that he was not going to win on defense, so he went on the offensive.

"By Saturday," *Golf World* magazine wrote, "Ben had given up the idea of out-smarting architect Jones and the new bunkers which had been excavated in places scientifically calculated to catch the tee strokes of long hitters unable to thread needlelike fairways with a golf ball. There was nothing for Ben to do but slug it out with the course, toe to toe."

The day broke warm and sunny, "a Texas day," Hogan said presciently as he prepared to tee off in the third round. He opened the round with birdies on the first two holes and added another in making the turn at three-under par 32, nearly inciting a riot in the process. Attendance was said to have been more than 17,000 that day, then an Open record, and when Hogan hinted at a final-day comeback, the throngs abandoned leader Bobby Locke and began following Hogan.

A script would have had Hogan routing the field over the final thirty-six holes. Of course, the Open never follows a script, instead requiring perpetual improvisation, and Hogan stumbled. The kind of putt that would bedevil him in later years, forcing him from competition, tripped him at 14, where he missed a four-footer for par.

The following hole featured a vexing bunker in the center of the fairway, copied from the Principal's Nose bunker on the Old Course at St. Andrews. Hogan's attempt to steer clear of the bunker resulted in the kind of debilitating shot that crippled him early in his career, a wild hook that sent his ball into a stand of trees left of the fairway, the first of six strokes he required to complete the hole.

In one two-hole stretch, he had undone all the positive work he had achieved to that point of the round, erasing his three-under par with a bogey and double-bogey. He also bogeyed the seventeenth hole and finished with a one-over par 71 that he was certain was the death blow to his chances.

The hangdog look he portrayed as he came off the course betrayed his mind-set. "He looked like a man condemned to die," one writer wrote. Only Bobby Locke's own troubles provided Hogan a stay of execution. Locke shot a 74, allowing Hogan to move within two strokes of the lead, news that energized him. En route to the first tee for his afternoon round, Hogan looked at Joe Dey and said, "I'm going to burn it up this afternoon."

Only a man of Hogan's skill could envision reducing to rubble a course that brought out the worst in men, even Hogan. Through fifty-four holes, not a single player had broken par. Hogan being Hogan was the factor working for him, and the reason that "the greatest mob to ever follow a golfer was at [his] heels as he played that final round," according to *Golf World*.

In the afternoon, Hogan went out in even-par 35, then began his theatrics by hitting a two-iron to within five feet of the hole at the tenth and holing the birdie putt. Dan Jenkins once wrote that "a good one-iron shot is about as easy to come by as an understanding wife." On that basis, an understanding wife is only marginally more difficult to come by than a good two-iron shot, and Hogan executed one while toting the burden of attempting to win back-to-back U.S. Opens.

Still one-under for the round, he came to the fifteenth, the ticklish hole that had deflated him earlier in the day. This time, he chose to lay up short of the bunker. He hit a three-wood from the tee, then another three-wood to the green, the ball stopping five feet from the hole, resulting in another birdie.

When he arrived at eighteen, the consensus was that he needed only a par to win the tournament. This time, he took the fairway bunkers out of play by leaning on his driver and blowing it past the potential trouble spots. His second shot stopped fifteen feet from the hole, and he made the putt for his second consecutive Open victory.

Of 418 rounds played that week, 412 of them were played over par, second in Open history at the time to the 424 over-par rounds played at Oakmont Country Club in 1935. The scoring average for four rounds was a frightful 77.23.

The severity of the test and his grade of A-plus required an appropriate summation, and Hogan delivered again. "I am glad," he said for posterity, "I brought this course, this monster, to its knees."

Writer Dan Jenkins recalled it somewhat differently, according to Detroit *News* columnist Joe Falls. "It sounded more like, 'I finally brought the !!#$%*&!# to its knees,' " Falls wrote.

Jenkins called it the finest round ever played. He and Hogan each hailed from Fort Worth, Texas, and were friends, but their bond had not unduly influenced Jenkins's analysis in defining the round. He offered statistical support. "The average score of the field that afternoon at Oakland Hills was 75," he wrote. "In that sense, you can say that Hogan's 67 was actually eight-under par on what he would call 'the Monster'—and it *was* the last round of the Open, right? Case closed."

Even Hogan recognized that it was something other than another day at the office. "Under the circumstances," he said, "it was the greatest round I have played. I didn't think I could do it. My friends said last night that I might win with a pair of 69s. It seemed too much on this course. It is the hardest course I ever played."

His was one of only two sub-par rounds played that week; Clayton Heafner shot the other, a final-round 69 that elevated him to second place. Hogan's winning score was 287, falling in the range that Jones said would be acceptable ("286 or higher").

Afterward, Jones's wife, Ione, approached Hogan and congratulated him on his victory. By then, any inclination he might have had toward a grateful acceptance of her warm gesture had been eroded by her husband's work. "Mrs. Jones," Hogan replied, "if your husband had to play golf on the courses he designs, your family would be on the breadline."

Hogan concluded that it was the greatest test of golf he had ever encountered, according to a *Golf World* magazine report in 1951, but not the finest test. His argument was that the fairway bunkering eliminated an elemental skill from the equation—that of attempting to hit the tee shot to the side of the fairway, giving him the most propitious entry angle to the green. At Oakland Hills, the goal was simply to hit the fairway, rather than a particular side of the fairway, as required in a quality design, as he defined it. He also noted that the target for the tee shot was smaller than it was for the second shot.

"Most of the experts agreed," wrote *Golf World*, "that the fairways are so narrow and so bunkered in the driving target area, a player has to try for the center with a prayer his ball will be on any part of the pretty."

"Hogan," Jones wrote, "never did concede that it was a good course, but he later admitted that he might have won more Opens had he been able to play them on more Trent Jones courses. To me, that's the ultimate compliment. Hogan's victory at Oakland Hills confirmed my opinion that only a great player can win on a great golf course . . . and I suspect that deep in his heart Hogan feels the same way."

Gene Sarazen, who tied for thirty-fifth, surely voiced a minority opinion at the time, when in a letter to the USGA, he described Oakland Hills as a masterpiece. "It was a challenge to the players," he wrote. "The best players finished on top."

The course was deemed eminently fair inasmuch as the Open indeed identified the best player, who was required to use every club in his bag over thirty-six holes on the final day. The point was made by William C. Fownes Jr., whose father had founded another Open course—Oakmont Country Club, outside Pittsburgh. Fownes said to Walter Hagen, "Walter, surely it isn't asking too much of the champion to require him to play every shot."

Snead's earlier assessment that Oakland Hills was "a nightmare" was a harbinger, as John Garrity noted in *Sports Illustrated*. "Neither Snead nor the golf writers realized that they were voicing one side of an argument that would rage for the rest of the century, he wrote. Oakland Hills in '51—long, tight, and overgrown with dense rough—represented the USGA's first effort to contrive a U.S. Open course of unsurpassed difficulty."

The public was enamored with the difficulty confronting the best players, presenting the first evidence that the USGA's efforts indeed provided revenge on behalf of golfers at large. "Much controversy has been raised by the treatment of the course, and it looks as if it is a subject that will be continued far into the future," Oakland Hills's general chairman John O'Hara wrote in a letter to the USGA. "The reception given Robert Trent Jones at the presentation ceremony showed that the public regards him as a hero. I am wondering whether the general rank and file of golfers, as well as spectators, feel that golf is difficult for them and they would like to see some of their obstacles placed in the paths of stars."

Nearly a half-century later, when the Open again was returning to Oakland Hills in 1996, British writer James Cusick coalesced the USGA's original laboratory experiment with Oakland Hills into a tidy, brilliant summary. Cusick wrote in the London broadsheet *The Independent*:

> *Bertrand Russell, bright but without a decent golf handicap, thought the infliction of cruelty with a good conscience was a delight to moralists, and that was why they invented hell. The United States Golf Association in 1951 must have thought the eternal inferno was a soft option. Instead, it created Oakland Hills.*

3

OLYMPIC METTLE

The San Andreas Fault is nature's impending revenge on the most eccentric of states—California—its tectonic plates creating tension expected to escalate one day, culminating in an earthquake that Californians have in advance dubbed *The Big One*. In the process, it has been suggested (no doubt wistfully) that California will wash out to sea.

Now, presumably the number of those seriously possessing a rooting interest in a catastrophe of this magnitude is not large, though it may include those residing in Western Nevada, standing by to inherit beach-front property. Yet, if The Big One is inevitable, there are those surely who would prefer its epicenter be located along the portion of the San Andreas Fault that cuts beneath the second, third, fourth, and fifth holes of the Lake Course at the Olympic Club in Daly City, California, on a bluff above the coast west of San Francisco.

These vindictive types would be professional golfers—at least those who have had to endure the Olympic Club's brutality in any of the four U.S. Opens played there. If Quake Corner, as that stretch of holes is called, were ground zero, the Lake Course might be put out of their misery.

The Lake Course at the Olympic Club is among the finest courses in the country, the principal qualification for U.S. Open consideration. Moreover, the USGA, once (and often still) perceived as a staunch practitioner of eastern elitism, was attempting to expand its presence in the West by taking the Open there on a more frequent basis. Only a trio of West Coast courses were deemed of a sufficient quality on which to stage an Open. One of them, Riviera, hosted the Open in 1948 and stumbled, allowing record scores, which might explain why the Open has never returned there. Another was the North Course at Los Angeles Country Club, where a haughty membership that refused to allow celebrities to join was disinterested in inviting the world onto its premises—policies, incidentally, that still exist.

The third, the Chosen One for the 1955 U.S. Open, was the Lake Course at the Olympic Club, the oldest athletic club in the country, founded in 1860 by a group of twenty-three men interested in physical fitness. Later, the Olympic Club became prominent for sending athletes to the Olympics, twenty-two alone to the Paris games in 1922. When the club decided to expand the activities it offered to include golf, it leased the Lakeside Country Club and eventually purchased it, at which point Sam Whiting was asked to redesign it in its entirety. It reopened as the Lake Course in 1927.

The membership at the Olympic Club is a curious lot. "It is cosmopolitan," the renowned golf writer Charles Price wrote, "historically significant, tastefully zany and baroquely beautiful. Like the city itself, it is the sort of place you like both to visit and live in. No member ever resigns from Olympic, even if he moves to Mozambique. He just dies and somebody else takes his place."

Even though the members call themselves Olympians, they strive not to take themselves too seriously, at least in the company of other Olympians. Self-deprecation is an art form at Olympic, demonstrated by a story that has become part of Olympic lore. A pair of members were playing in different foursomes one day and each repaired to the bar at Olympic and began bemoaning their play that day.

"I must be the worst golfer in the world," one man said between sips of a martini.

"No, I am," the other man said.

An argument ensued, so they agreed to match scorecards to settle the matter.

"What did you have on the first hole?" the first man asked.

"An X," the other man replied. "I picked up."

"See," the first man said, "you're already one-up."

The higher the profile, the more inviting the target. The baseball legend Ty Cobb was a member at Olympic, and in the First Flight of the Club Championship one year, he encountered a precocious twelve-year-old.

"I just killed him," said Bob Rosburg, who in adulthood became an accomplished professional who won the PGA Championship in 1959. "It was something like 7 and 6. The members gave him a pretty bad razzing. He didn't play there much after that."

It is instructive to remember that Olympic does not tolerate pedestals; those who arrive on one aren't likely to depart on one, as time would bear out.

Over the years, it became evident that the Lake was a special course, one that required the golfer to execute all manner of shots, a prerequisite to inclusion in the pantheon of great courses.

The Lake Course was ingeniously built on the side of a hill overlooking Lake Merced, its holes stepping down from the peak of the hill toward the lake, then back up again. The result is a topographical nightmare, from the golfer's perspective.

The inimitable Mac O'Grady, whose mind races in similar contours that are difficult to follow, played in the Open at the Olympic Club in 1987 and summed up the twists and turns this way: "The inclinations and topography of the Olympic Club disturb the vestibular semicircular canals of my inner ear-balancing centers." The English translation: "This," O'Grady said, rapping on a table top in the Olympic clubhouse following one of his rounds, "is the first flat surface I've been near today."

It is a course on which an Open performer, Jim Thorpe, once had a two-foot downhill putt and confessed to lagging the ball to the hole, a hedge against three-putting from tap-in range. He rolled the two-footer up to within inches of the hole and tapped in from there.

Fog is another feature that contributes to Olympic's difficulty by keeping the air damp and the course soft, effectively stretching it to troublesome lengths. The course begins on a ridge above the coastline and sits in the path of the daily summertime intrusion of the meteorological phenomenon that has branded San Francisco as Fog City. Accompanying the fog are bone-chilling temperatures that were at the heart of Mark Twain's assertion that the coldest winter he ever spent was a summer in San Francisco. Twain, incidentally, was a member of the Olympic Club.

"Here's the typical summertime forecast in the Bay Area," San Francisco weatherman Joel Bartlett said. "Fog along the coast, extending inward, night and morning hours, clearing back to the coast by the afternoon."

The fog frequently affects only the first two holes, which sit atop the ridge. As the course descends toward Lake Merced, the fog bank passes overhead. Fog on the first hole is an obstacle through which the members routinely play. "It's like playing a golf shot in pitch darkness," said Sandy Tatum, Olympic's club champion in 1956. "You're standing over your golf ball, and it's apparent that you're probably not going to see where the darn thing is going to go."

Olympic Club's head professional, Jim Lucius, said, "I basically live in fifty-eight-degree weather here in the summer. You can always tell the tourists. They're the ones who get off the plane wearing tank tops and shorts in June, July, and August."

If the USGA could have figured out how to dial up the fog and cold on demand, it might have thrown that at the players in 1955 as well. As it was, it seemed as though Joe Dey was still irritated that Riviera acquiesced to the manifold skills of Hogan and others in 1948 by failing to provide them an adequate test, and that he was determined that the course would fight back the next time the Open returned to the West Coast.

Among his initial instructions to the staff at the Olympic Club was to begin allowing the rough to grow in the fall of 1954, a full nine months before the Open was scheduled to be played there. "He didn't think we could grow rough there," said Bob Roos, an Olympic Club member and the general chairman of the '55 Open.

Ed Lowery, a member of the USGA Executive Committee and the area's USGA representative (and, incidentally, the ten-year-old truant who caddied for Francis Ouimet when he won the U.S. Open in 1913), mischievously suggested to Roos that they demonstrate to Dey that rough indeed would grow there. To do so required that they keep the mowers idle. "When Joe came out a few weeks before the Open, he almost flipped his lid," Roos said.

"What," Dey asked incredulously, "have you done to my golf course?"

Roos noted that USGA instructions then called for the first cut of rough to be two to three inches high, the primary rough to be six inches tall. There were no instructions beyond the primary cut; Olympic Club officials chose to permit the perimeter of the rough to grow unchecked. "It was a hayfield," Roos said. "We didn't cut it at all. That's why the scores were so high. If you hit it more than twenty feet off line you were up to your ass in grass."

Rosburg returned to the Olympic Club to play in his first U.S. Open in '55 and was aghast at the depth of the rough. "The rough almost got out of hand," he said, surely interjecting the *almost* to give his old club the benefit of the doubt. "It was brutal."

Sandy Tatum, a future USGA president, said simply that "Roos decided to make it pretty close to impossible."

To assist him, Roos summoned Robert Trent Jones, who, based on his work at Oakland Hills and Baltusrol, had already established himself as the Open doctor and the man called whenever an Open course required a difficulty transplant.

Jones held a genuine fondness for the Olympic Club, demonstrated by his lack of tinkering with the layout. He appreciated quality, even delivered by others, and expressed a disinclination to radically altering the work of great architects from the past. That did not mean that the work could not be improved upon to some minor degree, however. "The Mona Lisa," he once said by way of explanation, "will never be altered, but she wouldn't win the Miss America contest today."

The primary manner in which Jones made over Olympic was by extending it 300 yards, to 6,727 yards. This time, Jones added only one fairway bunker at the sixth hole, the lone fairway bunker on the course. A notable part of Jones's work throughout his career is characterized by his fairway bunkering, yet Jones actually removed fairway bunkers at Olympic.

This was good news to Roos, who believed that Olympic was more difficult without fairway bunkers to impede the progress of an errant shot that was headed for the trees, the great equalizer on a course without water hazards and fairway bunkers.

Trees define the Olympic Club; it contains upwards of thirty-five thousand of them—principally eucalyptus, pines, and cypress—and they collectively stand sentry at Olympic, guarding against errant shots that might otherwise avoid trouble, the bane of the golf course architect. O. B. Keeler took note of the mangled cypress tees and wrote that they "look as though they had been designed by a man who had gotten drunk on gin and tried to sober up on absinthe." Harvie Ward lost a ball in one of those cypress trees during the '55 Open there. Years later, when the tree was cut down, it was said to have yielded more than a hundred lost balls.

The easiest way to increase Olympic's difficulty without altering its elemental design, Jones concluded, was to extend some of the green-side bunkers to allow them to guard at least portions of the fronts of greens. "I thought Jones did a wonderful job," Roos said.

The length of the course suggested that the architect ran out of room, thereby forgoing a hole, say, a 400-yard eighteenth that would have stretched it over 7,000 yards, to full-sized. Instead, it was compact, by professional standards, measuring 6,727 yards for the '55 Open.

Hogan called it the longest short course in the world, based on its modest length, which belied the difficulty of a course deriving whatever length it had largely on the basis of long, difficult par 4s, and the fact that the grass is perpetually wet as a result of its proximity to the coast and the persistent fog. Lucius called the second through sixth holes "probably the hardest five-hole stretch in championship golf." In '55, the second measured 423 yards, the fourth 433 yards, the fifth 457 yards, and the sixth 437 yards. The lone par 3 in that stretch was long as well: 220 yards.

The longest, toughest par 4, the 461-yard seventeenth, was in fact a par-5, for the members. Dey, however, wished to avoid three finishing holes, offering only short-iron approaches to the green. His solution was to turn the seventeenth into an impossibly difficult par 4.

"It was wrong to play it as a 4," Roos said. "Nobody could reach the green with an iron, except Snead, who could reach it with a one-iron. Everyone else had to use a wood."

Jones concurred with Roos's assessment. He once called the USGA's decision to play the seventeenth as a four-par "a trick design" and "unfair to the player who strikes a good tee shot," an assessment born out by the 4.923 scoring average on the hole that week.

Olympic had short holes, too, all of them subtly difficult. The eighteenth hole measured only 337 yards for the '55 Open. Ostensibly, it was an easy finishing hole, requiring only a short-iron second shot to the green. But it featured a small, narrow green that sloped severely from back to front. Any approach shot left above the hole was looming disaster.

Of the eighteenth green at Olympic, Jones wrote: "If the hole is cut on the front portion and your shot winds up on the back plateau, getting down in two putts definitely requires God to be on your side."

A trio of bunkers that front the green seem to form the letters IOU, the course's mocking promise to repay you for the misery it has put you through.

Misery was not an adequate description for the wordsmiths bearing witness to its malevolence. Jim Murray called the Lake Course "the John Wilkes Booth of golf courses," as well as a "Bolshevik of a golf course."

It was, however, generally regarded as eminently fair. Ben Hogan even called it his favorite Open venue. "That's a pretty good testimonial from one of my heroes," Lucius said. "It's a golf course that has withstood the test of time."

The practice round typically is a low-key affair, an opportunity for the players to gauge how the course is playing and to develop a game plan. It is not a platform that routinely invites a temper tantrum, yet one in particular erupted, anyway. Ed Furgol had won the Open the year before, on the Lower Course at Baltusrol. On the final hole of his final practice round at Olympic, the defending champion hit his second shot into the small, but steep bunker fronting the eighteenth green. His attempt to extricate the ball failed when it caught the lip of the bunker and rolled back toward him. For his next swing—indeed, his next twenty-plus swings—he requested a nine-iron, then began an angry staccato drumming of the offending lip of the bunker, his intention being to rehabilitate it so that it would not commit a similar crime against reason in the days ahead.

Gene Littler was Bob Rosburg's houseguest in nearby Palo Alto that week, and the pair engaged in a practice-round game at Olympic, a dollar a stroke. Littler was among the favorites to win the '55 Open, though it was not evident by his play that day. He shot an 88, a number more often ascribed to an Olympic member playing to a fifteen handicap, and paid his room and board in the form of a gambling debt. Meanwhile, Jack Fleck, an obscure club pro from Davenport, Iowa, shot an 87 in a practice round.

Olympic was that kind of debilitating setup, a course so difficult that it might have fooled Trent Jones into underestimating it. Jones predicted a winning score of two-over par 282 based on his computation, hole by hole, that Olympic was playing to a par of 70.5, or a half-stroke over par.

When the tournament began, the weather was shockingly perfect, sparing the field further humiliation. "On the eve of golf's Great Adventure," *Golf World* wrote, "the elements relented and lifted the king-size bushel basket of fog that had been placed over San Francisco, permitting the worried athletes a welcome peek at blue sky and sunshine."

Sunny and warm may have prevailed, but neither was an adjective used to describe the collective disposition of the field following the first round. Eighty-two of the 162 golfers to start failed to break 80. Sam Snead holed a twelve-footer at eighteen to avoid joining that crowd. The host pro, John Battini, a man who presumably understood the nuances of Olympic Club better than any in the field, shot a 96. The scoring average was 79.8, a figure more likely to turn up in the club championship.

"Since the memory of modern man runneth not to the contrary," *Golf World* wrote, "there was never a first-round day the like of it in Open history. The crying room at Olympic was filled with wailing and gnashing of teeth."

Only a single 3 was made at the brutal par-4 seventeenth, by Al

Besselink. Ben Hogan, bidding to become the first in history to win five U.S. Opens, failed to reach the green in two. He completed his round in 72 strokes, then sarcastically noted that, "I played a par round today. Par *is* 72, yes?" No.

The rough demonstrated a callous disregard for the players' egos. Furgol missed one fairway by only five feet and was unable to find his ball in the rough. One caddie who had entered the deep rough in search of a ball set down the bag he was toting and had a difficult time relocating it.

Then, there was the case of Verne Callison, an accomplished amateur from Sacramento who would ultimately win two U.S. Public Links championships. Callison had an unplayable lie that required he take a drop. It was his misfortune that he was required to drop the ball in Olympic's gnarly rough. In those days, protocol demanded the ball be dropped over the shoulder, in effect, dropping it behind you. Callison properly made the drop, the ball settling deep into the thick grass behind him. When he turned to inspect the lie he had caught, he was unable to see the ball. A frantic search failed to turn it up and he incurred an additional penalty for a lost ball.

"That's true," Callison's widow, Carol, said. "That was back in the days when the USGA tried to make the players look as stupid as possible."

Only the tempestuous Tommy Bolt solved the riddle, doing so with his putter. Thunder Bolt, as he was known, needed only 25 putts and had eleven one-putt greens, enabling his temper to remain in seclusion, at least until he read the newspaper the following morning. He took exception to one account of his three-under par 67 (the only score of par or better in the first round) and initially declined to speak with the media following his second round. Of course, a seven-over par 77 in the second round was instrumental in depressing the mute button as well. Moreover, his tee shot at the eighteenth had caromed off a spectator and alighted in a bush, leaving him with an unplayable lie that required he return to the tee to hit again. Bolt nonetheless was tied for the thirty-six-hole lead, matching Harvie Ward, while Fleck, Hogan, Julius Boros, and Walker Inman each was a stroke back.

On Friday, under more blue skies, Olympic again showed its mettle. The scoring average in the second round was 78.9, only marginally better than the day before. Only three players bettered par: Fleck, Boros, and Snead. The cut was fifteen-over par 155, the highest in relation to par since 1941.

The final thirty-six holes were played in a single day then, and when the field completed the third round on Saturday morning, Hogan had positioned himself to win an unprecedented fifth Open, despite taking bogeys on the final three holes. Though he had yet to play a round in anything better than two-over par 72, he had opened a one-stroke lead over Boros and Snead. Fleck was a distant sixth, 3 strokes behind.

Only an historical victory lap around the Olympic Club remained for Hogan, who accomplished what was required of him—a round of even-par 70 that seemingly gave him a lock on the championship. Former star Gene Sarazen was working as a commentator for NBC and sidled up to Hogan to congratulate him. Sarazen in fact signed off the air by announcing that Hogan had won the Open. Certain, too, that he had won, Hogan flipped his ball to Joe Dey. "Here, this is for Golf House," he said, referring to the USGA museum in Far Hills, New Jersey.

Hogan had teed off an hour earlier than his lone challenger at that point, an unknown club pro. Jack Fleck's history suggested that he was not up to the task of delivering quality golf under U.S. Open pressure while attempting to topple the great Ben Hogan in his bid to make history. Fleck had never won a tournament of any kind and had earned just $2,700 in fifteen events in that, his first year on tour.

Meanwhile, a marshal, George Tomkins, kept Fleck apprised of Hogan's progress throughout the round. When Hogan had finished and Fleck was playing the fourteenth hole, Tomkins said to him, as though it were a fait accompli, "All you need is 1 birdie in the next five holes to tie Hogan." A birdie to tie Hogan down the stretch of an Open was a formidable task, but one that did not account for the other possibilities. "You know," said Littler, Fleck's playing partner, "he'll also have to get a few pars."

Instead, he threw in an immediate bogey, leaving him four holes in which to record two birdies to tie Hogan. To do so according to golf's Richter scale would have represented The Big One. Fleck nevertheless countered his bogey on fourteen with a birdie 2 on fifteen.

Hogan, meanwhile, had repaired to the clubhouse and was handed a celebratory Scotch and water. A man came in and announced that Fleck had parred 16. On which hole, a reporter asked Hogan, did he think he had won the tournament? A few minutes later a man came in and announced that Fleck had parred seventeen.

A weary Hogan stood up and went to take a shower. A tie seemed more than he could bear, given that it would require that he return the following day for an eighteen-hole playoff. His legs, never the same following the automobile accident that nearly claimed his life in 1948, were heavy from tramping around the damp hills of Olympic all week.

A victory for Hogan seemed more likely at that point, given his pursuer's predicament. Fleck was required to play his second shot at eighteen from the first cut of rough, to an exceedingly small green, and he needed a birdie to tie Hogan on the final hole of the U.S. Open.

The odds weighing heavily against him, Fleck pulled from his bag a seven-iron and managed to hit a high, soft shot that stepped only eight feet above the hole. Bob Rosburg later called it "the most amazing shot I've ever seen." Fleck then calmly holed the tricky downhill putt for a birdie that sent the tournament to an eighteen-hole play-off on Monday.

When Hogan emerged from the shower and began dressing, he had heard the crowd near the eighteenth green, adjacent to the clubhouse, erupt in a loud roar as Fleck's putt dropped.

"The kid's sunk it," a reporter said.

Hogan frowned. "I was wishing he'd either make a two or a five," he said, either of those numbers allowing him to go home rather than to engage in a play-off. "I was wishing it was over." Hogan then turned to a clubhouse attendant and motioned toward his clubs. "We might as well get those things back in the locker," he said. "We've got to play tomorrow, it looks like."

The headline in the *San Francisco Chronicle* the following morning unwittingly captured both the collective disappointment of a multitude of golf fans as well as the magnitude of the potential upset. UNKNOWN GOLFER BIRDIES LAST HOLE TO DEADLOCK BEN, the headline read.

Writer Dan Jenkins had called Hogan's final round of 67 at Oakland Hills the best round ever played, given that the average score of the field that day was 75 and that it was the final round of the Open. Well, Fleck also shot a final-round 67 and the average score of the field *that day* was 76.6, and he did so with birdies on two of the final four holes, including one at eighteen, to tie the intimidating Hogan. The case could be made then that Fleck's 67 was better even than Hogan's 67 four years earlier.

It certainly was the more remarkable of the two rounds, given the freak nature of it. Fleck was from Davenport, Iowa, an occasional tour pro and a full-time club pro at a pair of tumbledown municipal courses, Credit Island and Duck Creek, where greens fees were seventy-five cents. He had driven to the Open, a trek that took him forty-nine hours. He was said to have had three dollars to his name at the time.

Fleck also reckoned that he was the worst putter in history. "Everyone says that about himself," Fleck said, "but with me it was the truth." Yet, in the midst of his second round, he encountered an unusual feel in his hands, as though they had been touched by Kismet. Suddenly, the putter felt like magic and he began putting with the kind of confidence he had never known before. He did not three-putt the remainder of the tournament and spoke of the mystical "power" that guided his hands.

Hogan and Fleck each completed seventy-two holes in seven-over par 287, equaling the score with which Hogan won the '51 Open at

Oakland Hills. The stroke average for the field for the week was 78.72, the highest since World War II. More over-par rounds had been shot, 413, than in any Open since 1935.

On the morning of the play-off, Fleck was calm, perhaps from naïveté. He asked a friend whether the play-off was match play or medal play. "Medal play," the friend said, apparently hiding his disbelief at the question he had just heard. "You play just like you did yesterday."

Fleck encountered Hogan in the clubhouse, walked up to him, and offered his hand.

"Ben," he said, "I want to wish you well out there today. I was coming into El Paso when they were taking you to the hospital in that ambulance. We passed each other, and I didn't even know it was you. So I want to wish you well today. Good luck and play well."

"Thank you very much," Hogan replied. "Good luck to you."

The rough would have one final say in determining the champion. Hogan was one down when the duo arrived at the final hole of the play-off. Fleck hit a perfect tee shot. Hogan, however, pulled his tee shot into the thick rough, a victim, as it were, of Dey's meddling.

"His foot slipped," Roos said. "What happened was that when Dey came out before the tournament he thought some of the tees were uneven and he made us put sand on them. Hogan slipped in the sand at eighteen."

From the middle of the fairway, Fleck briefly considered his advantage, a one-stroke lead with Hogan in trouble. "We still had some more time to play," he told *Golf Digest*, "but after he hit it in the rough, naturally you figure he's going to have a little difficulty." When Fleck glanced over to see what kind of lie Hogan had, he was unable to see the ball. "Nobody had ever seen rough like that before," Fleck said. "I suppose it was close to a foot deep in places." Hogan decided that his only means of escape was sideways. When Fleck glanced over again, Hogan was aiming straight for him, causing him to retreat thirty yards back up the fairway, to escape harm's way.

Those up by the green watched intently as Hogan flailed his club a couple of times, sending weeds and grass flying. They presumed that he was taking practice swings, when in fact, he was taking strokes in earnest, attempting to return the ball to the safety of the short grass. Eventually, he holed a twisting twenty-foot putt that the crowd thought was for par, but it was in fact the culmination of a double-bogey six that enabled Fleck to win by three in an upset that continues to resonate across time, the upset that deprived Hogan of the record fifth Open title he would never win.

Olympic had shown its mettle. Hogan was a magnanimous loser. "First, I would like to make one thing clear," he said at the awards presentation ceremony. "There is nothing unfair about this golf course. I have just witnessed one of the greatest displays of guts and courage on the golf course that I have ever seen."

Years later, Hogan was said to have acknowledged forfeiting an advantage he held by his simple presence, that of intimidating an opponent, particularly an untested one. Early in the play-off, Fleck drove his ball into the rough, then encountered difficulty escaping. Once he reached the green, he was said to have apologized to Hogan. "Sorry to keep you waiting."

"That's OK," Hogan reportedly replied. "We've got nothing else to do today."

Hogan felt that this one instance of cordiality put a nervous opponent at ease. The story perhaps is apocryphal. Fleck has often said that it was not true, that it was fabricated by a golf writer, then passed down through the years, until it became part of the historical record.

Fleck need not have apologized for toppling a legend. He simply outplayed him. A quality accurate ball striker, Fleck expertly avoided placing himself in dubious positions and he putted beautifully. "Straight drives and good putts, isn't that how you win the Open?" he said.

The legend of American golf writing, Herbert Warren Wind, was there and was puzzled by the result.

"Who is Jack Fleck?" he wrote. "If you had been able to answer that question a week ago on a television quiz and had been able to answer it correctly, there is no knowing how many refrigerators and home freezers it would have won you."

Even Fleck himself recognized the prohibitive odds against his ever winning the Open, even using them to keep his household budget in check. "When I ask him for something for the house or myself," his wife, Lynn Fleck said in the aftermath of her husband's Open victory, "he'd always say, 'Wait'll I win the Open.'"

Fleck's young son Craig regretted only that his daddy had defeated the man he'd otherwise have been rooting for. "I'm glad Daddy won," little Craig said, speaking, perhaps, on behalf of the masses, "but I didn't like it that Hogan lost."

The irony is that Fleck was one of only two players using Hogan signature clubs, the other, of course, being Hogan himself. Hogan, in fact, was one of Fleck's idols. When his son was born in 1951, he wanted to name him Snead Hogan Fleck. His wife, Lynn, vetoed the name. Fleck countered by asking her to select a name from a list of U.S. Open winners. Craig Fleck was named for Craig Wood, winner of the Open in 1941.

Afterward, a tired Hogan hinted that he might be through with playing competitive golf at a championship level, that the work ethic he required of himself to prepare was too steep a price to continue to have to pay. "I don't think I can go through that again," Hogan said. "And that's not discouraging talk. It's that damned preparation. From now on, I'm a pleasure golfer."

The Olympic Club had taken its measure of a legend, as it generally did. It was not the sort of place where one could flout his credentials and expect to be extended courtesies reserved for the privileged. Those who arrive on a pedestal . . .

Hogan was the victim of an upset at Olympic. Arnold Palmer blew a seven-stroke lead with nine holes to play in the Open there in '66 and lost to Billy Casper in a play-off.

Tom Watson lost by a stroke to Scott Simpson in the '87 Open there—three of the best players in history, scarred by Olympic.

Rick Reilly in *Sports Illustrated* once called the Olympic Club the only par-70 cemetery, without considering how haunting a place it really was.

Fast forward to 1981. Bing Crosby's son Nathaniel, an accomplished amateur, reached the thirty-sixth hole final of another USGA national championship at Olympic, the U.S. Amateur, and trailed his opponent, Brian Lindley, by a considerable margin early in the afternoon eighteen.

This was a concern to ABC Sports, which was televising the final and was not scheduled to come on the air for another ninety minutes or so, at which point the match conceivably might already have ended. Bob Rosburg, working for ABC, was following the match with a producer and suggested that they begin taping the match in the event it ended early.

"We were walking up the seventh hole, in the right-hand rough," Rosburg said, "when suddenly I stepped on something. I couldn't tell what it was. I reached down and picked it out of the rough and it was a pipe, identical to the one Bing smoked."

Crosby had died four years earlier.

"The first thing that hit me," Rosburg said, "was that maybe the old man was around. I thought, 'boy, this is an omen.' "

Crosby immediately launched a rally and eventually defeated Lindley, one-up.

It was an eerie reminder that, when the USGA is involved, there is no telling what might be lost in the rough, even—as Hogan learned on the final hole of a play-off in 1955—a U.S. Open championship.

4

BLAST FURNACE OPEN

SOUTHERN HILLS COUNTRY CLUB, 1958

Tulsa, Oklahoma, in the summer, is a sweat stain, or, to borrow a phrase that Tommy Bolt once used to describe himself in a fit of pique, "hotter than a depot stove." Tulsa is located in the middle of nowhere, though its deep-fried denizens prefer to say that it is situated in the middle of everywhere. Where it sat, in fact, was atop a gusher; the city is a byproduct of the black-gold rush, an oil boom that once gave Tulsa its identity as the oil capital of the world.

Heat and oil are a combustible combination that fits comfortably into the United States Golf Association's scorched-earth policy that governs the U.S. Open, requiring the decimation of the field. Not satisfied with taking players' blood, it decided to ask for their sweat as well. The USGA wants its Opens won with an abundance of strokes, apparently including even those of the heat variety.

So it agreed to take the Open in 1958 to Tulsa, to Southern Hills Country Club, an oasis of manicured and irrigated rolling hills that sprang from the hardpan on the heels of the Depression.

Oil money was a renewable source, of course, and was easier to come by than other sources of investment capital. In 1934, members of the Tulsa Country Club became concerned that once the club's lease expired it would become a public facility. They resolved to build a new course and start a new club, and for assistance turned to Waite Phillips, scion of the family that founded Phillips Petroleum and a generous man whose benevolence was such that he was dubbed Tulsa's Fifth National Bank.

Phillips agreed to donate 360 acres of his own land south of town, provided the club raised $150,000. Phillips gave the members a deadline of eighteen days to raise the capital, and though they came up $1,000 shy, he agreed to proceed with the project.

For an architect, Phillips chose one of those with whom he frequently had conducted business and presumably was the most comfortable—a banker, naturally. Actually, he was a former banker, Perry Maxwell, a golf aficionado who counted among his friends Francis Ouimet, the 1913 Open champion from Boston who at twenty triggered the American golf revolution by beating a pair of British stars, Harry Vardon and Ted Ray.

Maxwell had left banking to pursue a career designing golf courses and had even assisted Alister Mackenzie in building the Augusta National Golf Club. Maxwell agreed to design Southern Hills for a fee of $7,500.

Among Maxwell's virtues was that apparently he had been an honest banker, which is reflected in his personal code that "if you always tell the truth, you don't have to remember what you said." He, too, was honest to his architectural philosophy. "First," he said, "you need a suitable piece of land, then you do as little to the land as possible. In this way, you give it character and you make it different from any other golf course."

Maxwell also knew that a golf course of the highest caliber could not sustain so lofty a standing without an adequate water supply to counter the oppressive heat of a Tulsa summer. Greens in Oklahoma typically were of the sand variety in those days and beneath the standards he sought. More than $50,000 was spent on drilling wells and installing a pipeline to transport water about a mile to the club's swimming pool and a retaining lake.

The fact that a world-class golf course could be built on a diminutive budget which, even by the standards of the day, was considered cheap was a testament to Maxwell's minimalist style.

The course was built principally with manpower and horse power, which provided a built-in deterrent to moving too much dirt around. Only one tractor was used, and though Maxwell and his crew wore it out—it was used for scrap metal once the course was completed—he did not perceptibly alter the landscape on which the course took form.

Even the undulations in the greens were subtle and contrary to Maxwell's one idiosyncrasy which came to be known as Maxwell's Rolls: greens with confounding peaks and valleys.

Southern Hills fits the definition of a classic design, one that requires all modes of transporting the ball. Of the fourteen fairways, eight require a right-to-left flight pattern, a draw, off the tee. Six require a fade. The ability to accurately work the ball in either direction is a foundation for stardom in golf and a requisite to playing Southern Hills well.

Nearly two decades later, Sandy Tatum, chairman of the USGA's Championship Committee, wrote of Southern Hills that "it has all kinds of character and lots of great change-of-pace holes. There are lots of places on this course where a golfer is confronted with a decision of whether to be bold or conservative. The bold play is rewarded if the golfer can bring it off. But he is severely penalized if he cannot."

A straight drive occasionally would work at Southern Hills, but tended instead to run through the fairway and into the rough, and the USGA, adhering to form, narrowed the fairways and allowed the rough to grow to penal proportions. "The course presented an arrange-ment of fairways as narrow as [Tommy] Bolt's four-wood," Dan Jenkins wrote, "and a Bermuda rough that was not only calf-deep but as gnarled as Tommy's temper could be."

Bolt, an Oklahoma native familiar with Southern Hills, knew it as a great test of golf before any tinkering was done to it. "They really let the rough grow [for the Open]," he said. "The fairways, and I'm not kidding, were thirty yards wide. We almost had to walk single file."

It was called "pitch-out rough," a forte of the USGA. Pitch-out rough is so long and thick that advancing the ball forward to any sig-nificant degree is a virtual impossibility at worst and a risky venture at best. The only viable alternative is to pitch the ball laterally, back to the safety of the fairway. "I can't tell you how many strokes I sacrificed pitching out sideways with sand wedges, trying to keep from making sevens," Bolt told *Golf Digest* years later.

The writer Herbert Warren Wind wrote of "the way a golf ball hit into the five-inch Bermuda-grass rough bordering the fairways invari-ably slipped down through the wiry, twisting blades and onto the ground itself, making a recovery shot with any club but a sand wedge practically impossible."

Bob Rosburg said the rough was worse than it had been at the Olympic Club three years earlier. "It was the worst rough I've ever seen," he said. "Bermuda rough. The ball would go right down to the bottom. It was enticing in a way. It looked like you could hit it out, that it wasn't too tough. Then you'd swing and the ball would go sideways."

Southern Hills's parameters—which also included small greens baked by the tremendous heat to a golden brown and hard as brick—suggested the winner would be the kind of player capable of demon-strating patience in the face of adversity certain to afflict everyone in the field. The parameters suggested the winner would not be Tommy Bolt.

He was called Thunder Bolt, Terrible Tempered Tommy, and Tempestuous Tommy, monikers he obtained by virtue of his notorious temper and its fuse that was only marginally longer than a shadow at noon. His tantrums were legendary. He once broke both his putter and his driver in the same round, which he immediately realized was not good course management. "Never break your putter and your driver in the same round or you're dead," he said, his words becoming an enduring part of his biography.

Jimmy Demaret said that "Bolt's putter spent more time in the air than Lindbergh." One apocryphal story has Bolt giving a clinic, when he invited his fourteen-year-old son to "show the nice folks what I taught you." The boy was said to have pulled out a nine-iron, muttered an epithet, and flung the club down the fairway.

Bolt's most famous toss came at the 1960 U.S. Open at Cherry Hills, when his driver betrayed him once too often and he flung it into a pond by the eighteenth green. A photographer captured his windup for posterity, a photograph without a shelf life. It resurfaced in publications again when the Open was returning to Southern Hills in 2001.

He recognized his own expertise at delivering a miscreant club down a fairway and offered a piece of advice for those similarly unable to maintain control of their tempers. "If you are going to throw a club," he said, "it is important to throw it ahead of you, down the fairway, so you don't waste energy going back to pick it up." He also said that he probably held the distance record for every club in the bag.

He routinely broke clubs, as well. Another apocryphal story has him arguing with his caddie about club selection for a particularly long shot. The caddie, the story goes, insisted it was a six-iron.

"A six-iron?" a puzzled Bolt said. "Why a six-iron?"

"It's the only club you've got left in your bag," the caddie was said to have replied.

Bolt tempestuously created the caricature and routinely reinforced it. He even looked the part. "I've got a face that looks like every time I miss a shot I got to do something about it," he once said. Jim Murray wrote that his face had been *lived in*.

He missed fewer shots than most, though his accounting was circumspect. "Me again, huh?" Bolt said once, peering at the heavens after missing a costly short putt. "Why don't you come down here and play me? Come on, you and your kid, too. I'll give you two a side and play your low ball." He once reckoned that he could make every putt for the rest of his life and still would not be even.

Bolt's temper overshadowed his talent, which was substantial. He was an expert ball striker who counted Hogan among his admirers. The question was always whether he could maintain the even keel necessary to allow his skills to flourish.

At the Open at Southern Hills, the uncharacteristic calm with which he had been playing that year remained with him, as though destiny already had written the script and that it had Bolt winning. He carried with him a small card on which the now ubiquitous Serenity Prayer was written: "God grant me the serenity to accept the things I cannot change, the courage to change the things I can, and the wisdom to know the difference."

"I just decided golf wasn't worth breaking a blood vessel over," he said, explaining the peace of mind he inexplicably had found. "So I relaxed. And I'm a different man."

"Tommy," Murray wrote, "was in the throes of one of his repeated reformations that year. Tommy saw the light more often than [renowned evangelist] Aimee Semple McPherson in those days."

The PGA may have helped by appointing Bolt to chair its good-conduct committee, in effect making him responsible for levying fines for aberrant behavior. He was his own first violator, fining himself one-hundred dollars for throwing a club.

His only memorable outburst the week of the '58 Open was directed toward a reporter for the Tulsa *World*. The paper noted Bolt's age as forty-nine, though he was in fact thirty-eight. The reporter, under whose name the error appeared, attempted to explain to Bolt that it was a simple typographical error. An even-tempered man surely would have accepted this as a plausible explanation and would have dismissed the matter. Bolt, on the other hand, is not a name that is synonymous with "even-tempered." Predictably, he was enraged.

"Typographical error, hell!" Bolt bellowed. "That was a perfect four and a perfect nine."

Murray noted that Bolt ended the week with the same number of clubs with which he began it. "None of them," he wrote, "orbited the Will Rogers Turnpike that week."

This was a remarkable demonstration of self-control by a man who heretofore had none, playing a course capable of trying the patience of a monk. The greens were cut to three-sixteenths of a inch, causing approach shots to skid. The rough was ankle-deep, four inches in height, and disinclined to allow an iron to pass through it without grabbing it by the hosel and twisting it closed. Even the sand was mischievous; one writer described the deep bunkers as having been "filled with ladies' bath salts." The sand was so fine that Patrick Abbott lost a ball in a bunker when the ball plugged and the sand filled in around it.

The sum of the parts created a riddle that only Bolt failed to find puzzling. He birdied the first hole by making a fifteen-foot putt, a good start by anyone's definition, but an omen from Bolt's vantage point. "The instant it fell in the cup I knew those other guys were all playing for second," he said years later. "It just felt that way. All I had to do was keep the clubs in my hands and finish. That's just how complete the control was on my emotions and how happy I was with the world. That's the way you have to be."

Even the stifling heat worked to his benefit; it helped alleviate the pain from arthritis in his back and neck, enabling him to swing freely. "While everyone else was sweltering and falling by the wayside," he said, "I just kept grinding."

The final flourish to an extraordinarily difficult course was provided by the wind, gusting to twenty-five miles per hour, blowing hot air and providing the '58 Open with its appellation, the *Blast Furnace*

Open. The day the tournament started, June 12, still has the highest low temperature for that date in recorded history in Tulsa, seventy-seven degrees. The following day set another record for highest low, eighty degrees. Each day established Tulsa's existing record for average mean temperatures for those dates: eighty-seven and eighty-nine degrees, respectively. The tournament began with the temperature ninety degrees in the shade and ended with the temperature surpassing one hundred.

It was a discomforting week on every front and it began, not surprisingly, with a pileup in the first turn, a crash of historic proportions. The first round produced some of the worst golf in Open history from a scoring standpoint. The entire field of 159 players shot over par and 79 players failed to break 80, resulting in an astronomically high scoring average of 79.7. The leaders were Bolt, Julius Boros, and Dick Metz, each of them shooting a one-over par 71. "Those scores are damned good, I'll tell you that," said Ben Hogan, who shot a 75.

The criticism was immediate and barbed. Gene Sarazen called the course ridiculous and recommended capital punishment for the man setting the pins. He particularly disdained the par-3 eighth hole. "That's the worst damn three-par hole I've ever played," he said, after posting a double-bogey 5. The hole's designer, Perry Maxwell, once called it his best par 3. "It looks so simple from the tee," he said, "that everybody will go for it, but if the ball isn't exactly on line, they'll take a 5."

Hogan had played the course literally hundreds of times while in the service and stationed in Tulsa during World War II, and was instrumental in convincing the USGA to bring the event to Southern Hills. Yet even he was taken aback, suggesting that a committee be formed to confront the USGA with its protest in an attempt to ensure that it not happen again. "This course is tougher than Olympic," he said. "Not better, but tougher."

"Man, this is the toughest golf course I've ever seen," said Dutch Harrison, the Arkansas Traveler. "The only way to play it is to stay in the locker room out of the heat and dream about the score you'd like to shoot."

This apparently was the approach taken by Byron Nelson, the one man who was not convinced that Southern Hills was that difficult. Easy for him to say. Nelson, of course, had already retired from competitive golf and was observing from a vantage point outside the ropes. "The course just doesn't look that tough," said Nelson, who with a bad back had scores of 72 and 73 in a pair of casual rounds at Southern Hills a week before the Open. "They can say it's the Open and all that for those scores, but I just don't know."

Similar conditions bedeviled the players in round two, a marathon event. A typical refrain from the Open is the length of time required to complete rounds prior to the thirty-six hole cut. The number of players in concert with the deficient skills possessed by a vast number of them, plus the difficulty of the course even for the game's best players, ensure long, tiring days. Never timid, Bolt was willing to deliver this message this time around. "It's been a long time since breakfast," he said, following the second round. "I wonder if [USGA executive director] Joe Dey has been out there five hours without eating. There are too many guys in the tournament who have no chance of winning. A hundred of them. They ought to keep the field to about forty players for this one. I think the Masters has the right idea."

The Masters, however, was an invitational, privately run, and kept its field to a manageable number. An Open is just that—open—and the fact that the national championship was at stake required a larger field, however overmatched much of it was.

It should be noted that Bolt did not come by his opinion without it having been a provocation; he had concluded his second round with a swell of anger that was certain to manifest itself in some form. He had three-putted the eighteenth green, making a double-bogey 6 that kept him from breaking par. He stormed away from the green, declining to talk with reporters. "Jim Gaguin [PGA field secretary] will do my talking for me," Bolt said. A cooling-off period of forty minutes removed the edge, however, and Bolt, sitting on a one-stroke lead, eventually emerged to meet the press.

He alluded to his calm demeanor. "I can make a mistake and not let it bother me," he said, though his disposition in the immediate aftermath of his double-bogey at eighteen said otherwise. "If I'd just had some food in my stomach on that last hole, I wouldn't have made that six. I just wanted to get food."

Bolt's second consecutive score of 71 gave him a one-stroke lead over South African Gary Player, whose second-round score of 69 was the only sub-par round in thirty-six holes.

Hogan played better, but still shot a three-over par 73 which inflicted damage to his ego, but left his sense of humor intact. Asked whether he was hurting, he replied, "Heck, fellas, I'm getting old. The day I turned forty I started hurting all over and have ever since."

The scoring average for the second round came down only marginally to 78.5, and the cut claimed Sam Snead, who shot rounds of 75 and 80. It marked the first time in his career, spanning eighteen Opens, that he had missed an Open cut.

Bolt had one of only three sub-par scores in the third round and opened a three-stroke lead. He closed with a 72 and won by four by playing precision golf on a course ill suited for it.

The par-4 twelfth hole, for instance, measured 465 yards and it was brutal, featuring a narrow fairway with a dogleg left. A bunker ominously sits on the left side of the fairway, in the hinge of the dogleg, as a deterrent to those contemplating taking the shortest route to the hole. The alternative is an iron from the tee and veering right of the bunker, which leaves a long and difficult second shot over a stream with a stone bank to a small green. Predictably, it was among Hogan's favorite holes, given the sharp-shooting required to play it well. Even today, it is considered among the most difficult holes in golf. It was responsible for much of the distress Southern Hills caused the players that week.

Bolt's mastery of the twelfth propelled him to victory; he birdied it each of the first three rounds and parred it in the final round. "The son of a bitch played twelve in three under," Dutch Harrison said, shaking his head in wonderment.

Later, he said that when he birdied the first hole of the tournament, he was convinced that he would win, that the golf course as battlefield had been transformed into his own Elysian fields. Even when his driver betrayed him, as it often did that week, he never punished it, though he was considering a replacement for the final round. "This would be a heckuva time to change horses," Lloyd Mangrum told him, convincing him to continue using the same clubs that had staked him to a three-stroke lead.

Never a particularly good putter, Bolt nonetheless found the range that week. Even when on the green, rules then permitted a golfer to leave the flagstick in, which Bolt chose to do, and it paid dividends, he said. "I just kept leaving those flags in," he said. "Those little old flimsy sticks couldn't keep the ball out and they helped you draw a straighter line."

On the final two holes, Bolt was in such good humor and so certain of victory that he conversed with a group of reporters who had filtered out onto the course to watch him complete his incredible journey. Before each shot, he'd eye a writer he knew and predict what he intended to do with the shot. This went on through his final putt at eighteen.

"When I consider how treacherous the game of golf is and how often a seemingly insurmountable lead can vanish as quickly as a puff of smoke," Herbert Warren Wind wrote, "I am still aghast when I recall Bolt and company indulging in this strange repartee on the closing holes. It surely must stand as one of the most bizarre triumphant marches in sports history. Of course, it might have been the heat."

Bolt was a wire-to-wire winner, his seventy-two-hole score of three-over par 283 providing him a four-stroke victory in one of the most difficult Open tests ever. Hogan called it the toughest course he had ever played, though he stopped well short of calling it the best. His own performance was curtailed by a wrist injury incurred when he attempted to muscle a ball from the rough during a high-stakes practice round with Bob Rosburg and Claude Harmon. Hogan was given an injection to alleviate the pain, according to George Matson, the club's unofficial historian, who has worked at Southern Hills since the '40s. "Hogan just didn't have the feel of it," Matson said. Hogan tied for tenth at fourteen-over par.

The scoring average for the week was 77.92, second only, since World War II, to Olympic Club's average of 78.72 three years earlier. The par of 70 was broken only five times. Bolt was the only player without a score of 75 or higher on his ledger. This Open produced an identical number of over-par rounds recorded at Oakland Hills in 1951, 412.

It could have been worse. Thirty minutes after the tournament ended, a hailstorm battered the course, severely damaging the greens. Had the storm struck a day earlier, the course would have played substantially more difficult, if indeed it had been playable at all.

The '58 Open, incidentally, was the only major championship Bolt ever won. He had the requisite skills to win majors, but lacked the equally requisite temperament.

Four years later, incidentally, the man called Thunder Bolt and Terrible Tempered Tommy filed for divorce from his wife, Mary Lou.

He cited, among other reasons, her temper.

5

BOSTON MASSACRE

Apair of British players, Wilfred Reid and Ted Ray, were at dinner following the second round of the 1913 U.S. Open at The Country Club in Brookline, Massachusetts, outside of Boston, where they engaged in a spirited political debate that ended when Ray stood suddenly and unleashed a right cross that landed squarely on Reid's nose. A stunned Reid, blood streaming down his face, attempted to stand to defend himself when he was struck again.

A waiter intervened, stopping the bout, but the damage already had been done. Reid, tied for the lead at that point, was no longer a factor in the tournament, shooting rounds of 85 and 86 the next day to finish fourteen strokes back. He couldn't stop the bleeding, as more than one wag had noted, invoking a shopworn phrase to describe a round gone awry.

The United States Golf Association is keen on remembering anniversaries, and its explanation for taking the Open back to The Country Club at Brookline in 1963 was to commemorate not this two-punch affair, but the fiftieth anniversary of Francis Ouimet's dramatic victory there. Ouimet (pronounced WE-mut), twenty, was an amateur who lived across the street from The Country Club's sixteenth green and knew the course intimately from a decade of having caddied there. Ouimet had played only through the benevolence of his employer, John Morrill, from a local sporting goods store. Ouimet had already used his vacation time to play in the U.S. Amateur and was in no position to ask for additional time off to play in the Open. Morrill, however, was perusing the Open pairings in the newspaper one morning and noticed that Ouimet was entered. Morrill felt that since Ouimet had entered, he ought to fulfill his obligation by playing and instructed him to do so. In an eighteen-hole play-off, Ouimet toppled the British golf empire, represented then by Harry Vardon—clearly the best player in the world—and Ray, his touring mate and the 1912 British Open champion.

Ouimet's upset victory over the Brits inflamed America's passion for this game, which heretofore had been a foreign one and was an adequate reason, surely, to bring the Open back to The Country Club fifty years later. However . . .

The Ouimet story, we submit, simply served as a cover for the USGA's de facto motivation for returning the Open to Brookline fifty years later: To commemorate the first known case of a bloodied and bowed U.S. Open contender.

In this case, the golfer, Reid, was bloodied and bowed in a literal sense. The USGA is not without compassion; it will accept its Open participants be bloodied and bowed in a figurative sense as well. Its goal in every Open is to throw a knockout punch, and though it will not resort to violence to do so, it will respond with whatever means necessary. Even the weather, its haymaker in 1963.

A nasty winter and a miserable spring conspired to prevent tournament officials from bringing The Country Club up to the standards ordinarily required by the USGA. When the tournament began, strong winds heightened the difficulty of a course that even under normal conditions would have been debilitating for much of the field.

The Country Club was by reputation a brawler masquerading beneath the finery of the privileged. It was one of five clubs that formed the United States Golf Association in 1894, and its blood ran blue. Its aristocracy manifested itself in its name change. Brookline Country Club failed to allow it to stand out from other country clubs, so it became *The* Country Club, tingeing it with an air of superiority, in the manner of Britons referring to the British Open as *The* Open, or those who refer to New York's leading newspaper as *The Times*.

The attitude of the membership at The Country Club was perpetually haughty; more than one hundred years later, when the club announced that it would host the 1999 Ryder Cup Matches and the 2005 PGA Championship, it did so by posting a typewritten message in the men's locker room, as though it considered these events of no more importance than the next member-guest tournament, which similarly would be posted in the locker room.

At least it had a boast-worthy golf course. Actually, the Open course at Brookline was a compilation of The Country Club's three nines, seven holes from each of the Clyde and Squirrel courses, and four holes from the Primrose nine. It was designed in part by William Flynn, who routinely built three sets of tee boxes and was the first to label the closest set the forward tees, rather than the ladies' tees, to encourage short-hitting and elderly men to play from them without a sexist aversion.

The predominant feature that rendered The Country Club difficult was the dozen greens or more that could not be seen from their fairways. On one particular hole during his first practice round at The Country Club, Doug Sanders asked his caddie where the green was.

"Over there some place," the caddie replied, gesturing in a vague direction.

"Such is the topography," Arthur Daley wrote in *The New York Times*, "that this is a gigantic game of blindman's bluff because the target is hidden on the fifteen longer holes."

The greens were miniscule targets, frequently referred to as the size of postage stamps. The USGA saw to it that they were fast, too. "Trying to hold the ball on these greens is like putting on a flight of marble stairs and trying to stop it on the next-to-last step," former Open champion Julius Boros said.

The back nine was the fiercer of the two, particularly the twelfth hole. The USGA, form prevailing, transformed the twelfth from a par 5 to a 470-yard, uphill par 4 with a blind second shot over a hump. "The twelfth hole is ridiculous," Arnold Palmer said. "It's a par 5 and not too good a par 5 at that. I hit one of my good drives and a two-iron and I was short."

Players referred to the hole as the Hunchback of Notre Dame. Nicklaus called it "a par four-and-a-half, if there is such a thing."

Ed Furgol was no less frank in his assessment of the back side. "That second nine," he said, "should be declared a disaster area." He dubbed the ninth through the fourteenth holes as "the stretch of terror."

The rough was signature U.S. Open difficulty. "The greens committee apparently seeded it with barbed wire," Daley wrote.

"You can score here if you keep the ball in that mowed stuff," Jacky Cupit said. "This is a typical Open course. You've got to stay out of the rough."

Sam Snead deployed his inimitable Southern eloquence in describing the rough: "Man, that rough is really something. That ball goes a few inches off the fairway and you're in it. I mean, you're really in it. I'll bet the ball sinks into that rough six inches. I was in one spot and I really came out of there. I dug a divot that was big enough to bury a cat in. Just put in the cat, replace the divot, and build a monument."

Strength is an advantage for extricating a ball from deep rough, and Jack Nicklaus was born with a surplus of it. Gary Player took note of Nicklaus playing from The Country Club rough and marveled. "I've never seen anything like it," he said. "He just tore out grass, mud, and golf course. Didn't bother him at all."

This was among the reasons Nicklaus had to be considered a favorite to successfully defend his U.S. Open championship. Yet, Arnold Palmer declined to acknowledge him as such, perhaps the first volley in what would become a spirited—and, at times, contentious—rivalry. At the Open at Oakmont the year before, Nicklaus, twenty-two, had defeated Palmer in a play-off. Now Palmer was being asked to identify the players he favored in this Open. He cited Gary Player, Tony Lema, and Dow Finsterwald. No Nicklaus?

"I did forget him, didn't I?" Palmer replied. "I just wanted to see if you'd notice."

Predictably, The Country Club absorbed a profusion of verbal shrapnel from professionals who subconsciously may have recognized that their own skills failed to measure up to the challenge. Dow Finsterwald shot a 77 in a practice round, yet declined to join in the chorus of grumbling, a startling turn that compelled John Ahern in the *Boston Globe* to detail Finsterwald's sounds of silence. He wrote:

Dow Finsterwald had a practice round score of 77 and he didn't have a tantrum or even an unkind word. This makes Dow a man among men and definitely the silent partner in the vast group that heads out for the Open championship at The Country Club this morning. His silence was a lot more eloquent and a great deal more refreshing than the volcano of gripes emanating from the premises since Sunday.

Eventually, perspective has to emerge from the verbal rubble, and it came from a man who by rights ought to have lost perspective, as far as the Open is concerned. "We all play the same course," Sam Snead said, "and one guy can be as miserable as the next."

Asking them to ascribe a number in advance to their misery is standard operating procedure for the media, which perennially asks players to project a winning score. It is a futile exercise, giving the unknown variables that can send scores soaring either higher or lower. The consensus guess was 280, four under par, a number that surely would send the hitmen from the USGA into collective apoplexy. "Well," Snead, the wily veteran, said, "I'll take 284 and sit right here by my locker and be very happy about it."

The wind was the wild card, the difference between the golf course swatting away well-struck shots or embracing them. "That wind, should it come up, might make it a little rugged," Snead said. Paul Harney, a native of the area and familiar with the nuances of the course and the weather, predicted that should the wind stiffen, "I don't think anyone will break par."

Heat and humidity, mainstays of an eastern summer, arrived on cue for the first round and were accompanied by the dreaded wind, the menace that can quickly dissipate whatever benevolent tendencies a golf course has. Only six players equaled or bettered par in round one.

The *Boston Globe* was sufficiently moved by the havoc the wind created to quote Virginia Woolf: "The beauty of the world . . . has two edges, one of laughter, one of anguish, cutting the heart asunder."

Among those who realized the anguish were Carson Herron, the prototypical beleaguered, overmatched contestant in 1963. Herron, whose son Tim would become a PGA Tour winner more than thirty years later, was an accomplished player in his own right, a club pro from Minnesota who had qualified to play at Brookline. He opened the tournament with an 85 that left him dazed and pondering a career change.

"I just shot 85 and I still don't know what happened," Herron said. "I teach at a little club in Minnesota. I had to cancel my lessons to get here. I practiced all week and the members were very nice to me. It cost me four hundred dollars just to come here. I'm embarrassed to go home."

The first-round leader was Bob Gadja, a club pro from Michigan who went on to become part of an answer to a trivia question: Who were the only two players to play seventy-two holes in a U.S. Open without shooting in the 70s? One was Lee Trevino, who in 1968 had rounds of 69, 68, 69, and 69 to win by four. The other was Gadja, who shot a 69 to begin the tournament, startling everyone, then followed with rounds of 80, 84, and 80.

Champagne Tony Lema was two shots off the lead and wondered why he was so fortunate. "When you looked over the shot, you'd think the wind was with you," he said. "When you'd take your stance, it would be a crosswind. When you were in the process of swinging, the wind would seem to be against you. It was confusing." Lema, who once celebrated a victory by ordering champagne for those in the press room, was asked whether his generosity would extend to the Open press corps, were he to prevail here. Gauging the wind, the difficulty of the course, and his ability at that point in time to handle either, he suggested the writers would be better served by ordering it up them-selves. "Maybe we'd better not wait until I win," Champagne Tony said. "You might lose your taste for it."

The course played predictably difficult, even for the defending champion, Jack Nicklaus. His résumé already included victories in the Masters and the Open, and he was expected to renew his acquaintance with Arnold Palmer, whom he had defeated in the Open a year ago. But Nicklaus opened with three straight bogeys en route to a five-over par 76.

"What," he said to the media afterward, "do you want to know from a 76 shooter?"

Nicklaus had injured his neck in an earlier tournament, though he declined the opportunity with which the media presented him, to use the neck as an excuse. His only explanation was that he had attempted to alter his game to better fit a course that was more suitable to a right-to-left ball flight. Nicklaus's preferred flight, from years of fine-tuning it, was a fade, left to right.

"I'm disgusted," he said. "This is a very disappointing round. Nothing was bothering me but myself. I had my heart set on this for a long time, since the Masters, to be exact. I felt I had to make a change from left to right to right to left for this course. I did the same thing before the Masters and won there."

The following day was worse; Nicklaus missed a ten-foot par putt at eighteen, shot a 77, and missed the cut by a single shot, the last time he would miss an Open cut until 1985. "This is my worst Open," he said. "I've had worse scores, but then I didn't expect to do well. This year, I did. I never made a putt, which doesn't help."

The wind had picked up its pace, as though the USGA had ordained it so. Only seven players equaled or bettered par in round two. Palmer and Finsterwald each shot 69s, the best rounds of the day, and along with Jacky Cupit tied for the lead.

Palmer's criticism of The Country Club began and ended with the twelfth hole. He generally was fond of the course otherwise. "This is the first USGA Open course I've played that requires everything in golf from every standpoint," Palmer said. "This course requires a lot of shot-making ability and thinking. I've used every club except my one-iron, and there were a couple of times I could have used that. If I play as well the next two rounds as I have the first two I won't be disappointed."

A winning score of 280 no longer was viable. "If anyone does do that," Tony Lema said, "they'll have to cheat."

The twelfth hole adequately defended its honor, inflicting pain to varying degrees. It even took its toll on the *Boston Globe*, which in a fit of hyperbole likened the wreckage to the battle waged in the Revolutionary War slaughterhouse known as Bunker Hill. "Never since June 17, 1775," the *Globe* wrote, "have so many casualties been left strewn over a hillside in this vicinity."

On the final day, the wind took the tournament hostage and demanded that it play itself out the way a member-guest might, with one notable exception: Those in an Open aren't receiving handicap strokes. "We'd hit that ball up in the air, and never knew where it was going to come down," Boros said. The breezes gusted to thirty miles per hour.

"The lashing breezes, strong enough at times to knock the players off balance, made virtually impossible the precise shotmaking needed to conquer the 6,870-yard, par-71 layout," *The New York Times* wrote: "For every shot that strayed, a price had to be paid. It was exacted by high, dense rough that infringed on fairway and green, deep sand traps and beckoning lakes, ponds and brooks."

Palmer called it the worst wind he'd ever encountered. "The wind was difficult during the British Open in '61," he said, "but it was nothing like this."

Attempting to inject levity into the situation, Tony Lema said, "It's not tough out there. I only got blown down twice. Seriously, I never played a tougher golf course under tougher conditions."

Over thirty-six holes on Saturday, not a single player equaled or bettered par. The scoring averages in the final two rounds typically are considerably lower than they are for the first two rounds, when the field is laden with overmatched players. Once the cut is made and the USGA's definition of chaff is asked to leave the premises, scoring averages can be expected to descend. That was not the case at The Country Club, when the third-round scoring average of 78.2 was the highest of the week and the final round average of 77.4 was only a fraction below the opening-round average of 77.5. Twenty-six scores of 80 or higher were shot.

"These scores," Mason Rudolph said in summary, "look like a caddie tournament."

Sam Snead shot a lamentable 79 in the morning round, then delivered his lament: "This persnickety course isn't like the seaside courses we get in Britain. They're laid out for the wind with big greens. But this one has itsy-bitsy greens and the roughest rough I ever did see."

He broke for lunch, and he finished eating, he spotted Samuel H.

Wolcott Jr., the president of The Country Club, and gave him his unsolicited assessment of the course. "You've really got a monster out there," Snead said. "If I had my double-barrel shotgun here, I'd shoot it right between the eyes."

Surely he'd have missed, wrote *The New York Times* columnist Arthur Daley, noting Snead's diminished sharp-shooting abilities that day.

The Country Club was not similarly unarmed, to Snead's chagrin. He was in its crosshairs, reflected in his score of 83 in the afternoon round.

When Art Wall left the course after shooting a third-round 76, he considered himself to have been paroled. "I feel as though I'd just been in jail for five days," he said.

George Bayer, a behemoth of a man, was cut down to size by the conditions. He made an eight on one hole, a nine on another. "I don't care about the eight and the nine," he said. "I just want to get out of here alive."

Tommie Aaron, a future Masters champion, shot a twenty-over par 91 in the third round.

Cupit closed with rounds of 76 and 75 and still was part of the play-off, though ultimately he paid the steepest price by double-bogeying the seventeenth hole of the final round to squander a two-stroke lead. "These are the worst conditions I ever played in," he said. "It's worse than the snow at Pebble Beach [in January of 1962]. If the wind was consistent, it wouldn't be so bad. It's so tiring and you have to think so much and that tires you, too."

Palmer shot a 77 in the morning, the result in part of a triple-bogey 7 on the eleventh hole, when the wind knocked down his second shot and it alighted in the water. Palmer hit only eight greens in regulation and the score was his highest of the year. "This is ridiculous," Palmer said. "I shoot a 77 and I'm only one stroke off the pace. The funny part about it is that I said to myself as I walked up to the fifth hole, 'I'm going to shoot a 67 on this round.' It shows how silly a guy can get."

Palmer followed with an afternoon round of 74 that included his missing an eighteen-inch putt on the seventeenth hole. Ordinarily, shooting 151 over the final two rounds will earn you also-ran money. In this case, the course was playing so difficult that it earned him a berth in a play-off.

Boros assumed he had played himself out of contention with a third-round 76 that left him three shots behind the leader, Cupit, and two behind Palmer, Lema, and Walter Burkemo. He closed with a one-over par 72, equaling the low score of the final round, and was probably headed toward home, a notion he pondered over a medicinal beer in the clubhouse. "I was almost packed and ready to go when news of the tie reached me," he said. "This was amazing. I just couldn't believe what had happened. How in God's name does a guy who shoots only two birds all day get into a play-off?"

Boros, Cupit, and Palmer each finished at nine-over par 293, the highest winning score in an Open since 1935 and equaled the second highest winning score since 1929.

Boros was a large man, earning him the nickname Moose. His was never an accelerated gait down a fairway, in part from his size and its inherent anchoring effects and also his nature. His pastimes were golf and fishing, neither of which is served from a lack of patience. Yet once he got to his ball, he never dawdled, never pausing even to take the proverbial waggle with his club. "He was slowest and fastest," *Golf Digest* editor Jerry Tarde wrote. "Slowest walking to his ball and fastest once he got to it."

His swing was easy and rhythmic and the source of the title of a book he wrote, *Swing Easy, Hit Hard*. He was wired properly to handle what the Open required of those who would succeed, notably patience. He had won the Open previously, in 1952, at the Northwood Club in Dallas, and in a stretch of thirteen U.S. Opens, he finished in the top five on eight occasions.

Boros's easy manner and effortless swing were his advantage in an Open play-off, when pressure tends to quicken the pulse and the stroke, neither of which is conducive to producing quality golf shots. He took command of the play-off early, then squeezed the life from his opponents at the eleventh hole.

"Arnold Palmer was over in the woods to the left, giving a pretty good lesson on how to kill snakes," the *Boston Globe* wrote. "Jacky Cupit was in the right rough, the steel wool. Julius Boros was a little bit off line, too, about the length of a king-size cigarette from the middle of the fairway, and the big guy from Fairfield, Connecticut, looked for all the world like Humphrey Bogart."

Boros made his par, while Cupit made a bogey to fall five behind Boros. Palmer, meanwhile, had hooked his drive into a rotted tree stump, which, incidentally, *had not* deliberately been put there by the USGA, perhaps contrary to what some might have suspected. Palmer slashed at the ball twice without extricating it. His third attempt finally dislodged it. Ultimately, he made another triple-bogey 7 to fall 7 strokes behind Boros. One writer suggested that the eleventh be forever remembered as "Palmer's Purgatory," given that he played 19 strokes in three rounds there, seven-over par.

Eventually Boros, with a 70, would defeat Cupit by three and Palmer by six. He hit only ten greens in regulation, but his ability to save par from the prohibitive green-side Open rough enabled him to prevail. "I play that shot out of that rough around the greens pretty well," he said. "I always practice that shot for an Open. I cut it out of there with a wedge, like a sand shot."

Boros was a man whose demeanor might have been described as dull, but the *Globe* kept comparing him to stars from the entertainment industry. He was Bogart in one article and Perry Como in another. "Boros," according to the piece invoking the Como comparison, "seemed to use a minimum of effort and motion while shooting a one-under par 70."

Palmer's bid might have come unhinged the night before, when he became the victim of a stomach ailment. He was "perspiring heavily throughout the round and loaded with medicine," *Golf World* wrote. Even his charisma was suffering. After hitting a poor bunker shot at ten, he slammed his wedge into the sand. "He looked like a little boy who's afraid he's going to lose," the *Globe* wrote. "He got the razz . . . a loud bazoo."

"Arnold was my pigeon," Boros said years later. "I'd beaten him before. I usually did." Boros enjoyed chiding Palmer this way, even declining to admit that Palmer was ailing that day, as had widely been reported. "I think he was more sick about losing," Boros said.

Boros did not agree with the media's characterization of himself, either. "They called me lackadaisical, imperturbable, placid," he told *Golf World*'s Tim Rosaforte once. "*Sports Illustrated* said I won a spectacular Open in an unspectacular way. I didn't show much emotion. But inside I was the same as everybody else."

He *was* placid and a refreshing antidote to the typically belligerent behavior by many in the field, who openly detested a difficult course. They were scolded, too, by Bob Fitzgerald in the *Boston Globe*. In a story offering advice in the event the Open ever returned to Boston, he wrote:

To insure the happiness of the temperamental professionals it would be well to have a golf course with greens that are: one, not so huge as Oakmont's; two, not so tiny as The Country Club's.

You shouldn't have any rough within fifteen feet of the putting surfaces. If you have traps, be sure they are mostly decorative and not in position to penalize mis-hit shots.

And for goodness' sake, don't have any holes with blind shots.

All of this isn't guaranteed to keep the glamour boys happy, but it just might help.

You do all this, and maybe we can persuade the PGA to provide its members with little booklets explaining the difference between legitimate criticism and plain bad manners when they are guests at somebody's golf course.

Once again, the USGA successfully had brought out the worst in the players. Their collective grumbling resonated with the men in the blue blazers, who had achieved their goal in bringing the Open to Brookline. Indeed, the '63 Open was The Country Clubbing.

"The Old Lady of Boylston Street was able to cackle like the witches of Endor," Daley wrote in *The New York Times*. "Bubble, bubble, toil and trouble."

6

PASTURE POOL

Alfalfa once grew from the land on which Hazeltine National Golf Club was built in Chaska, Minnesota, outside Minneapolis. It was plowed under when construction on the course began in 1961, a lamentable lack of vision on the developer's part. Totton Peavy Heffelfinger was building Hazeltine with the intent of bringing the Open there, and, as a former USGA president, he ought to have recognized the potential for employing alfalfa as the primary rough, inasmuch as the USGA historically required players who missed the fairway to play their next from the hay, as tall rough routinely was referred.

The fact was that a good farm indeed *was* ruined when Hazeltine was built, as was suggested by an irate golfer when the Open finally arrived there nine years later.

Hazeltine was built on rolling farmland on which corn was also grown and cattle once grazed, providing fodder for professional golf's resident occupant of the critic's corner, Dave Hill. Asked what Hazeltine lacked, Hill replied, "Eighty acres of corn and a few cows."

Thus, the era of target golf was introduced, though not as the architectural concept it would later become. In this case, the targets were varied in form. One target was the left chimney on Heffelfinger's home, which Jack Nicklaus sarcastically recognized as the place to aim on one of many blind shots presented by Hazeltine National Golf Club. Another was Robert Trent Jones, Hazeltine's designer, who spent many summers dodging verbal bullets fired by disgruntled professional golfers who had come to view under-par scores as an entitlement.

The most perforated target, however, was Hazeltine itself, the most reviled course in the history of the U.S. Open, at least as it presented itself in 1970. This was the Open that introduced a variation to the golf term we know as *the chip*. Hazeltine gave us the *cow chip*, a euphemism for bullshit, the players' consensus opinion of Hazeltine, but also representative of Hill's view that the course would have worked better as a cow pasture.

The controversy framed the 1970 U.S. Open, essentially enabling the United States Golf Association to achieve its de facto definition of Nirvana: The course played the starring role, relegating the players, even the winner, to distant supporting roles. It so effectively did this, in fact, that the '70 U.S. Open assumed a prominent position in the pantheon of historically memorable Opens.

The man responsible for both Hazeltine National Golf Club and the Open debacle was Heffelfinger, the president of the USGA in 1952 and 1953. Past presidents of the USGA retain clout, and Heffelfinger used his to persuade the USGA to bring the Open to Hazeltine, a course without a history to extol its virtues, exposing it to inevitable criticism.

Hazeltine opened in 1962 and lacked the maturity that provides exceptional golf courses with their depth and character. More time is needed to adequately recognize a course's flaws and to have them corrected. Greatness is not assigned, as the USGA seemed to attempt to do with Hazeltine by awarding it the Open.

It had been designed by Robert Trent Jones, the Open doctor, who might have been sued for malpractice, had anyone considered the notion. Jack Nicklaus was first in line at the complaint window. In an article he wrote for *Sports Illustrated*, he protested the profusion of blind shots at Hazeltine. This elicited a memorable response from an agitated Jones: "Maybe Jack Nicklaus is blind." Jones also suggested that when Nicklaus penned his piece for *Sports Illustrated*, he had not yet seen the course.

Nicklaus was meticulous in preparing for major championships and had scouted the facility in advance of the Open. "When I played the course for the first time recently, I frequently felt lost," Nicklaus said. "Stepping onto several tees, I did not have a clue as to which direction the hole might be."

The blind shots require that golfers find a distant target on line with the green, and Nicklaus used Heffelfinger's farm as one on the eighteenth hole. "I hope they don't decide to work on Tot Heffelfinger's roof during Open week," Nicklaus said, noting that his target was Heffelfinger's left chimney.

"The only thing you can aim at on this course is two little clouds," another player muttered. "And if they move, you're in the lake."

The course was said to lack definition. "You tee it up at the first hole and all you see is lawn," one player said, "no way of telling how the hole should be played."

Hazeltine's reputation preceded it; the PGA Tour's Minnesota Golf Classic had been played there in 1967, providing players a sneak preview, with unflattering results. Lou Graham won the Minnesota Golf Classic with a score of 286, the highest winning score on the PGA Tour that year.

A story circulating before the '70 Open was that the USGA phoned Don January to inquire whether his entry had been lost in the mail. January was one of only thirty-five fully exempt players, so surely he had intended to enter, the USGA reasoned. "I didn't enter," January was said to have replied. "I don't want to play that course."

Frank Beard was an accomplished player and outspoken to a fault, a combination that made him attractive to editors. *Golf Digest* rewarded him for his candor by giving him a column. In one treatise on Open courses, he went off on Robert Trent Jones and Hazeltine. "Jones," he wrote, "is bound and determined to build courses that nobody can break 80 on, instead of great championship courses . . . Hazeltine is not a championship course. . . . Every hole is a dogleg, and you can't see what you're shooting at off the tee or to the green. On some holes the fairway bends left and the ground slopes right. The greens look as though somebody buried a bunch of elephants in them."

Bob Rosburg suggested that the course be plowed under. "Jones has so many doglegs on this course he must have laid it out in a kennel," Rosburg also said. Another player suggested the course had been designed by Lassie.

The doglegs, featured on a dozen of the holes (Hill said that even the par 3s had doglegs), asked of the players what Open courses typically caution against, that they gamble, by attempting to cut across the doglegs to substantially reduce the length of the holes. "The gamblers will be among the frontrunners," Nicklaus said. "You'll either have to cut across the doglegs or play long irons all day long as second shots. The par-5 holes are not going to be the usual birdie holes. You'll have to be precise with drives, much more than I usually am, more than many of the fellows. There are so many blind landing areas. Eleven greens are not visible from the tees."

Several of the longer players had decided to avoid some of the doglegs altogether, by deliberately hitting their tee shots into adjacent fairways, from which the greens were accessible from a shorter distance.

Even P. J. Boatwright, the USGA's executive director, found it difficult to defend the course. "It is a very hard course," he said, "but not great architecturally."

Criticism of an Open venue is an annual ritual, of course. "Dwelling on a golf course in previewing the U.S. Open is almost a must," *Golf World* wrote, "as most major championships find the players sharing the limelight with the course itself, as it should be." This time, it went beyond the pale. It was even called "Hiawatha's revenge against the white man."

"I saw some of the things that Rosburg said about plowing the place up," said Heffelfinger, the general chairman of the '70 Open, "but I'm not going to worry about it. I'm sure the majority of golfers enjoy playing our course."

In reality, it may only have been a minority of golfers, and a small one at that. One voice of dissent came from the diminutive South African, Gary Player, who ranked it among Robert Trent Jones's best work. Player always seemed to go against the grain on the issue of U.S. Open layouts. "This one has balance," he said. "This is what a U.S. Open should be played on, a real test of golf. It's the number-one tournament in the world, so the man who wins it should really have to play and earn it. And it's tough. This is what I call a course with character, because it is so well balanced. The holes are not stereotyped. On the par-5 holes, you will see more sixes than in any tournament I can remember for a long time."

Player perhaps saw the par 5s as an equalizer. A slight man without the strength and length of many of those against whom he was competing, Player typically was less likely to reach the green in two than his contemporaries, Arnold Palmer among them. "I don't think much of the par-5 holes," Palmer said. "They don't reward the good shots, because you can't get home on them in two with a truck. I can hit two great shots and the other guy might scrape a couple, but my only advantage is a shorter club to the green."

During a U.S. Open, on a course on which he left his fingerprints, Jones was required to play defense, as he was at Hazeltine. "If you want a wide-open golf course with flat greens and all flat fairways, you might as well order it from a Sears Roebuck catalog," he said. "An eighty is embarrassing to the pros and I sympathize with players competing under extreme pressure. But everything is relative. I think the criticism is unfortunate. It's sort of a vendetta. The players are accustomed to shooting in the 60s on easy courses. Their pride is hurt when they see their scores go higher. But that does not mean this course is not an infinitely fair—although difficult—test."

Only after years had softened his hard line, Jones acknowledged a flaw with the design, though he pawned it off on the developer's plans. "Heffelfinger . . . had insisted that a children's course be built alongside the championship layout," Jones wrote in his book *Golf's Magnificent Challenge*. "This required land we would have preferred to use for the regular course, adversely affecting four holes on the front nine."

The club took its name from the body of water near which it was built—Lake Hazeltine—though from the golfers' perspective a more appropriate moniker might have been Lake Woebegone, with apologies to native son Garrison Keillor's own Lake Wobegon. The tournament began under a cloud of controversy, which was provided an assist from winds gusting up to forty miles per hour and rain, rendering Hazeltine virtually unplayable for a woebegone field.

Winds were so strong that a large leaderboard was listing precariously and was shut down for the day. Players routinely backed away from shots, concerned that the wind might blow them off balance in mid-swing.

Sixty-seven players failed to break 80 in the first round. The scoring average was 79.1. Only one player broke par, England's Tony Jacklin, shooting a one-under 71. Jacklin was at ease in conditions ostensibly imported from home in Great Britain. "I'm used to the wind," he said, "and to tell you the truth, it wasn't tremendously strong compared to the wind we sometimes have in England. I'd like three more days like this. I really wouldn't mind if the weather stayed like this for the rest of the tournament. More wind wouldn't bother me a bit."

Arnold Palmer, ever the diplomat and unfailingly polite, initially was unable to summon a statement resembling reverence. "I don't know what to say," he said as he came off the course following a round of 79.

Once the first round had blown through, the grounds were littered with the debris of shattered golfers. An amateur, Pat Fitzsimons, played the first nine holes in 49, stood on the tenth tee, and said, "I'm not having much fun out here." Then he walked off the course and went home. Fortunately, the scars weren't permanent; five years later, Fitzsimons won the PGA Tour's Glen Campbell-Los Angeles Open.

Lee Trevino shot a 77. "I'm so hot I don't want to say anything," he said, though, predictably, he was unable to help himself. "At least I beat Gary Player and Jack Nicklaus, and if you beat those two cats, you can't be doing too bad." It was, however, too high a score to consider a down payment on the purchase he intended to make. When he won the '70 Open, he had said beforehand, he'd use the $30,000 first prize to "buy Texas and give it back to the Mexicans."

Trevino also beat Palmer, who was uncharacteristically demure in its aftermath. "I can't give you my general impressions because ladies are present," he said, once he had composed himself enough to share his thoughts. "Very frankly, I didn't do anything real well out there."

Dave Marr shot an 82 and deduced that he was two-over par. "That's counting 80 as par," he said, "which it really should be today."

It was as though Nicklaus, among others, had talked himself into playing poorly. He opened with an 81. When he encountered a reporter, he issued his famous rejoinder, "Excuse me, while I go throw up."

Later, he expounded on his round, which included an opening nine of 43. "After I had practiced in the wind," he said, "I felt I'd be happy with a round anywhere in the 70s. By the third hole, I told Orville [Moody, his playing partner] that an 80 in this stuff wouldn't be embarrassing. And by the ninth, I was beginning to feel that a man could shoot 80 and still win the tournament. I still feel that way."

Bill Hyndman, an amateur, opened with a respectable 76 and said he felt as though he had been in a fistfight. "The wind was gusting so strong," he said, "that it twice almost knocked me down."

Tommy Bolt was unable to contain his tempestuousness. He shot an 80, about which some reporters sought illumination. "Haven't you newspaper sons of bitches got something to do out on the golf course?" he said. He later said that he felt as though he were over par before hitting a single shot.

Columnist Jim Murray, in peak Open form, amusingly cloaked the first round of the '70 U.S. Open in historical analogy. "This U.S. Open," he wrote, "now has to rank with the great catastrophes of all time—the eruption of Vesuvius, the retreat from Caporetto, the sinking of the *Titanic* and the blowing up of the *Hindenburg*."

The counterpoint was offered by Jacklin, who frequently saw optimism, even when none existed, perhaps giving him an advantage over those who brought a negative mindset to the course each day. "You have to accept life as it is," he said. "Just because you don't like certain things, they're not going to be changed. That's my attitude towards golf."

The weather was mild on the second day. The wind had diminished almost entirely and the sun was out, an optimistic sign for one young woman, according to this report in the *Minneapolis Star*: "As [she] said to her male companion, at the third hole as both watched Frank Beard sink a twenty-five-foot birdie putt, 'I hope it gets real hot so I can take off my brassiere.' "

Virtually everyone was more comfortable on Friday. Twenty players shot par or better, and Jacklin had a two-under par 70 to take a three-stroke lead over Hill, who shot a 69 and ought to have been in good spirits as a result.

Instead, he was of a mind to vent.

The most outspoken critic of Hazeltine turned out to be Hill, a rancorous man who spoke his mind without regard to the possible repercussions. Hill was not interested in requiring that his thoughts go through an editing process en route to articulation. The words that came into his head just spilled out unimpeded by prudence, as they did when he played for the U.S. team in the Ryder Cup matches at Royal Birkdale in Southport, England, in 1969, and declared that he would never return there. "The next time I come over here," he said, "I will have died and my body would have been shipped to the wrong place."

He was brutally candid, which made virtually any question a loaded one.

Do you, he was asked after the second round of the Open, like the course better now that you have played it well?

"No sir," he replied. "If I had to play this course every day for fun, I'd find another game."

He was asked how he found the course.

"I've been trying to find it ever since I came to Minneapolis. Just because you cut the grass and put up flags doesn't mean you have a golf course."

What does the course lack?

"Eighty acres of corn and a few cows," he replied. "They ruined a good farm when they built this course."

What ought to be done to improve it?

"Plow it up and start all over again. The man who designed this course had the blueprints upside down."

Hill was curiously stoic when he delivered his assessment. He never raised his voice, instead allowing his words to pierce their target. "I've associated with idiots," Hill said, "but he [Robert Trent Jones] passes himself off as an intelligent man. My two kids could lay out a better course than this one."

Why hadn't he just withdrawn and gone home?

"I've done it several times," he said. "When I don't like the course or the people or where I'm staying, I pack it up and go home. If I didn't have friends around me here, I would have left Tuesday. We laugh a lot and drink a lot."

It should be noted that his judgment was not impaired when he delivered his pointed assessment of Hazeltine. His principal complaint was that several greens sloped away from the fairways, and that given the length of the course, players were attempting to hit long irons into greens inadequately designed to hold them. "It's impossible to make the ball hold," he said. "Although I won't enjoy it, I hit the ball higher than most in the field and it still bounces. You can imagine the problem the low hitters have. That's why Casper and Trevino are no huge threats."

Boatwright was informed of Hill's remarks and was angered by them. "A man is entitled to say what is on his mind," Boatwright said, "but how he presents his views becomes a matter of taste and good manners."

Hill's comments overshadowed Jacklin's performance and made him the story of the week. Minnesota, some might have submitted, was now the land of ten-thousand lakes and one flake. "Jacklin Boosts Lead but Hill Hogs Headlines," read one banner headline. Jim Klobuchar wrote in the *Minneapolis Tribune* that Hill had riled the PGA, the USGA, and the USDA (United States Dairy Association).

The following day, Hill was fined $150 by Joe Dey, the commissioner of the PGA Tournament Players Division, who issued this statement:

> *David Hill has been reprimanded and fined $150 for conduct unbecoming a professional golfer because of the manner of his criticism of the Hazeltine National Golf Club. In determining such matters, distinction is made between objective critical analysis of a golf course and the kind of criticism which tends to ridicule and demean the club. It is considered that Hill's criticism was of the second kind. The PGA Tournament Players Division regrets any embarrassment which has been caused to the club and the USGA.*

Hill's response to the fine? He took it in stride. "To me," he said, "a fine is just like a bogey. It doesn't mean that much. I expected the fine.

I'd get upset if somebody stepped on my ball, but not for something like this."

It was not his first fine. A year earlier, Dey had fined him $150 and demanded he write a letter of apology for cursing a PGA staff member at the Doral Open.

Hill said he wrote the check for his Hazeltine remarks the night before the fine was levied, anticipating that his statements would cost him. He, too, agreed that Dey had not erred in deducing that the comments ridiculed and demeaned the club, a rare instance of an athlete speaking his mind and not recanting the following day by employing the tiresome defense that his quotes had been taken out of context.

"Mr. Dey is a fair and honest man," Hill said. "He just told me I should find another way to express myself."

It was not bad advice, certainly, but it was wasted on Hill, a man given to telling the truth, as he perceived it anyway. "Some people don't like what I say," he said, "so I try to avoid them. I have tried not to be so outspoken. The press comes to me. I don't go to them. If you don't like the answers, don't ask the questions. I believe in answering all the questions from the press honestly."

Besides, he added, "I really wasn't mad at anybody except old what's-his-name."

That would be Robert Trent Jones, a bantamweight who continued to counter punch against heavyweight criticism. "I feel as if I've been hit by a bad shot," he said. He disagreed with the assessment that the course lacked definition, pointing to Hazeltine's myriad mounds, bunkers, and trees.

As for those infernal greens that slope away from fairways, Jones said, "A shot to a green that slopes away requires a little thinking." And doglegs? "I don't feel doglegs are bad. They don't make that much difference."

The abysmal performances of Nicklaus and Palmer, Jones explained, was a result of power hitters playing a course that overtly penalizes the occasional wildness that accompanies free swingers. "They need latitude and there is not much latitude here," Jones said. "Power has its rewards, but it also has its hazards. I think Nicklaus is a great enough player to play this course, but I think he came here with a negative attitude."

Dave Hill, incidentally, was serving as the spokesman for a cadre of disgruntled players, a few of whom offered to pay his fine for him. Another, Howie Johnson, advised him to make the check out for $300 to cover what he might say after the next round.

An argument could have been made in defense of Hill. Hill made a reasonable one himself. "Scores shot here by Palmer, Nicklaus, and Player do not compliment your course," he said.

Rosburg wondered aloud whether Jones could even break 100 on his own creation.

Fourteen players equaled or bettered par in the third round, not an unreasonable number by Open standards and an indication that when the course was not played in a wind tunnel it was not as severe as the players suggested it was. Jacklin shot another 70 and increased his lead to four over Hill, whose skill at playing Hazeltine belied his sentiments about the place.

"Us rabbits," he said, "can play down 101 and do all right," he said. "This course discourages them [Player, Nicklaus, Palmer, et al.] from the start. I'm not smart enough to get discouraged. I hit it, find it, and hit it again."

Hill continued to dominate headlines; third-round newspaper coverage centered as much on Hill's remarks and subsequent fine as it did on Tony Jacklin's lead. "Hell," Frank Beard said to Hill, "why don't you write a book to express your opinions? You won't make any money giving opinions to the press for free."

Jacklin was not even able to receive substantial press coverage at home; a newspaper strike in England limited the Great Britain press corps to a single writer, Leonard Crawley. "I've got all of England at my feet," Crawley said.

* * *

When Jacklin arrived at his locker before the final round on Sunday morning, he found a note taped to it. It said simply, "Tempo," and had been placed there either by Tom Weiskopf or Bert Yancey, he said. When Jacklin first arrived in the States to pursue a golf career, his swing tended toward quickness, an invitation for disaster in golf. Weiskopf, Yancey, and Bob Toski each provided assistance that helped him slow his swing down and provide it with the rhythm required of a consistent swing.

"I had trouble with a fast swing," Jacklin said. "Then one day I found it. Just like whistling. You blow and blow and finally one time a sound comes out."

Tempo was his swing key that day and he closed the tournament with a third straight 70 that enabled him to win by seven, the largest margin of victory in the Open since 1921. He also became the first Englishman to win the U.S. Open in fifty years. He became only the fourth player to lead, wire to wire, and the first since Hogan won the Open in 1953. His 72-hole score was seven-under par 281 and he had bettered par in all four rounds.

Hill succumbed quietly, but only in a figurative sense. His putter betrayed him in the final round and he finished a distant second. In a literal sense, he continued to make noise. Earlier that day, he said he should have driven a John Deere plow to the course. And his parting shot to Hazeltine? "If they can't do any better than this next year, they'd better fold it up."

Later, Boatwright, who a year before had replaced Joe Dey as executive director of the USGA, asked Hill what his organization had ever done to him to deserve this kind of treatment.

"You put the Open on this course," Hill said.

Hill originally had planned on boycotting the awards ceremony, which the runner-up is expected to attend. He relented, however, and showed up to a chorus of "moos" from a hometown crowd that had taken his farm references personally.

Time, and a $150 fine, failed to soften his stance. "I'll never play this course again," he said. "But I'll come back to Minneapolis if the tournament [the Minneapolis Classic] is held at another course."

For finishing second, Hill received a check in the amount of $15,000. It was unsigned, the USGA's own parting shot, inadvertent or otherwise.

Dave Hill remained steadfast through the end in his distaste for Hazeltine. The *Minneapolis Tribune* columnist Jim Klobuchar wrote: "Hill courteously signed all proffered programs and then, asked by an onlooker to deliver some suitable words of reconciliation so that all might depart in fellowship, he carefully removed his glasses and disclosed, 'My friend, I would not come back to play on this golf course for a million dollars. I mean if they guaranteed me a million dollars. The course was designed by a sadist. I'm talking about the architect, Robert Trent Jones. Jones hates golfers.' "

Twenty years later, Hill reneged on his promise. At the club's invitation, he returned to give the course a second chance, as it was being prepared to host the 1991 U.S. Open. He gave it his blessing.

When Warren Rebholz, executive director of the Minnesota Golf Association and president of Hazeltine National Golf Club, sent out his annual creative holiday card in 1990, it contained a picture of him kneeling in front of Dave Hill, pleading. "Please Mr. Hill," the card said, "say something nice about Hazeltine."

"Don't beg, President Rebbie," Hill's response read. "You're going to have a great Open on a great course."

<u>7</u>

BEAUTY AND A BEAST

PEBBLE BEACH GOLF LINKS, 1972

The end of the earth—from the perspective of those who considered Far Hills, New Jersey, home of the USGA, to be the hub of the universe—was once loosely defined as out west, which the USGA visited only reluctantly and as a means by which it could stage its national championships without having to argue on behalf of its use of the adjective *national*.

The U.S. Open was first played in 1895, yet was not held west of Illinois until 1930, when it went to Minneapolis. It did not venture further into the hinterlands until 1938, when it was played at Cherry Hills outside Denver.

The USGA finally made its first Open foray to the West Coast in 1948, to an outpost called Los Angeles. It shipped the Open west again in 1955 and 1966, to a frontier town known as San Francisco.

"Meanwhile," the *Los Angeles Times* wrote about Pebble Beach Golf Links, "for more than fifty of those seventy-one years one of the world's best courses served as nothing more important each June than a feeding ground for deer and a playground for amateurs."

At least Los Angeles and San Francisco each had an international airport and a burgeoning citizenry to whom the USGA could sell its tickets, justifying its presence there. When the subject of taking the Open to Pebble Beach was broached, those responsible for making the decision furrowed their collective brow.

Pebble Beach is located 120 miles south of San Francisco, 325 miles north of Los Angeles—or, as the USGA surely viewed it, somewhere between Sodom and Gomorrah—in what then was a sparsely populated way station on the California coast. The Monterey Peninsula was not yet the destination resort that it would later become, and the USGA was concerned that it was too remote to lure an adequate supply of spectators, creating a potential embarrassment and financial disaster for the organization.

"Pebble Beach was at the end of the world," said Frank Hannigan, the former executive director of the USGA. "We considered going to Pebble Beach for the '72 Open very risky. There might not have been anybody there. There were money concerns. We actually put into the contract that we had to receive a minimum amount of money no matter what happened. We got 65 percent of the admissions and 12 percent of the gross on programs. We had to make a minimum amount of money so we wouldn't go broke. That's the truth. We thought, 'people can't get to Pebble Beach.' The U.S. Amateur was played at Pebble Beach and nobody was there."

The meager crowds on hand to witness Jack Nicklaus's victory in the 1961 U.S. Amateur at Pebble Beach were among the USGA's principal counterpoints to the argument put forth by the Del Monte Properties Company, that it could project representative crowds based on the success of the Bing Crosby National Pro-Am played there each

January, often in inclement weather that nonetheless failed to detract from the large crowds that typically gathered.

The crowd factor was only the half of it. The USGA equally was concerned that the Pebble Beach Golf Links might be incapable of putting forth a true test of championship golf. There were those expressing doubts that it could fulfill the standards set forth by the USGA and deliver an Open-quality challenge to the best players in the world.

The Del Monte Properties Company failed to argue persuasively that the course was up to the task based on it holding its own when the professionals played at Pebble Beach every January. The Bing Crosby National Pro-Am was an important golf tournament, but not in the vein that the U.S. Open is. It was a party—the Crosby Clambake—built around a tournament, creating the perception that it was not especially serious. Moreover, the weather early in the year was often cold and nasty and entirely different from summer weather there.

"A lot of people said that Pebble Beach had a couple of good holes, but that it was not really a good test of championship golf," said Neal Hotelling, author of *Pebble Beach Golf Links: The Official History.*

It also was a public course, a fact that surely rankled a few in the USGA, who in borrowing a page from their USGA ancestry may have viewed the game as something less than an egalitarian one. The Open had never been played on a public course, in fact, and doing so would run contrary to how the USGA viewed its Open sites. How can you have hallowed ground when the public is invited to traipse across it day in and day out?

The USGA's elitist, myopic view failed to consider that Pebble Beach, although a public course, had an appropriate air of superciliousness with which high society could relate. The wherewithal of the well-heeled was a requisite to playing Pebble Beach. "Golf is not cheap on the Peninsula," the *Los Angeles Times* wrote. "At Pebble Beach the green fee is twenty dollars."

A laughably low green fee today—particularly for Pebble Beach— twenty dollars was prohibitive in 1972, and it gave Pebble the faint aroma of elitism that the USGA failed to recognize while it attempted to grapple with the discomforting suggestion that it play the Open on a public course.

The USGA diplomatically avoided saying so, instead taking the position that a membership was required to ensure an ample supply of volunteers, meanwhile disregarding the number of volunteers the Crosby employed each year.

"More to the point," Hotelling wrote in his book, "the USGA was uncomfortable with the thought of holding such a major tournament on a public-access golf course. It would take months to prepare Pebble Beach for a U.S. Open. The thought of just any old duffer taking div- ots just prior to the tournament was disturbing. A club membership would be much easier to control."

Obviously, Pebble Beach was not without assets, arguing forcefully on its behalf. It is the prettiest place in golf, a living postcard con- tributing to a magnificent stretch of coastline that Robert Louis Stevenson may or may not have called "the most felicitous meeting of land and sea in creation." He received credit for writing the sentence, though it has never turned up in any of his writings. The words, who- ever their author, resonated with truth.

Moreover, Pebble Beach already was at or near the top of Jack Nicklaus's pantheon of great courses. Nicklaus had won the U.S. Ama- teur there in 1961 and eventually would win three Crosbys there as well. Pebble Beach was also arguably the course with which the golf fan was most familiar, more so than Augusta National at that point. Pebble Beach had become familiar to the public through the annual telecast of the Crosby and its menagerie of stars from the worlds of entertainment and golf.

The components added to a course on which a major champi- onship ought to have been played, even after the negatives had been considered.

To alleviate the USGA's financial concerns, Aimee G. Michaud, president of the Del Monte Properties (which owned Pebble Beach Golf Links), finally offered the USGA a guarantee of $250,000, "the great hook," he called it. The year was 1968 and the USGA took his bait, swallowing hard and agreeing to bring the Open to the end of the earth in 1972, "on the condition," Hotelling said, "that they could prepare it for the U.S. Open. Some people were not comfortable with that."

In retrospect, the USGA ought to have considered the end of the earth the perfect venue for the U.S. Open, given the obvious hazard created by the distinction. At Pebble Beach, a player runs the risk of hitting it off the map, literally, further increasing the difficulty quotient. A significant portion of Pebble Beach represented, if not the end of the world, at least the end of the continent. In those days, eight of the eighteen holes were on the seaside, lending the course a substantial dose of its character and giving it a sliding scale of difficulty, depending on the strength and direction of the ocean breezes.

Pebble Beach Golf Links follows a rudimentary figure eight. The course begins with three inland holes (though they are not far removed from Carmel Bay), then reaches the water at number four. The fifth hole in those days was inland, with the course returning to the seaside for holes six through ten. It veered back inland for eleven through sixteen before returning to the waterfront for the final two holes.

"The only trouble with emphasizing the grandeur of the seaside holes at Pebble Beach," Herb Wind wrote, "is that this may promote the impression that the inland holes are rather ordinary. They are not. . . . The inland holes, with their emphasis on finesse, complement the seaside holes perfectly."

The course has never been appreciably long, but the greens are smaller than the hearts of the sadists on the USGA Executive Committee. Hitting these greens in a breeze is the equivalent of attempting to hit a small moving target—not with buckshot, either—but with a single bullet.

Jim Murray recognized Pebble's wretched nature and likened it to a pirate. He, too, wrote: "It's not a golf course, it's a hellship. At night, when the wind's in the rigging, you can hear the ghostly screams of bloodcurdling rogues who disappeared into a sand trap or down the seawall years ago. When the tide's out, you can see the rotting hulks of bagsful of Spaldings where they crashed on the rocks years ago."

The task of preparing the hellship was assigned by P. J. Boatwright, the USGA executive director, to a San Francisco attorney and formidable amateur player, Frank D. Tatum, better known as Sandy. Tatum had played in the 1947 U.S. Amateur and countless California Amateurs at Pebble Beach and revered the course and its roots. When he was attending Stanford, he worked at construction jobs in the summer to save enough money to play in the state amateur there. "I'd blow it all in one wonderful week at Pebble Beach," he said. "It was one of the most intelligent things I've ever done."

To ensure that he not inadvertently besmirch this national treasure, he sought the counsel of Jack Neville, the man who had designed Pebble Beach. Neville was eighty-one at the time, but still living on the Monterey Peninsula and still selling real estate for the Del Monte Properties Company.

"Together, Tatum, Boatwright, and Neville reinterpreted the course to bring into balance the original shot values given the improvement in equipment," Hotelling wrote, a reminder that reacting to technological advances in equipment has been a perpetual chore for the USGA.

Still, the only changes this group deemed necessary were superficial and principally dealt with the course condition and its bunkering.

In the winter prior to the Open, the USGA seeded the rough with fescue grass that deliberately went untended, eventually becoming exceedingly high and thick. In some places, the rough reached as high as a player's kneecap. The paying customers in the spring occasionally lost clubs in the rough, when they laid them down while using others to play a shot.

The poa annua grass on the greens was shaved, creating a concern that it had been killed by the USGA. Poa tends to blossom as the day wears on, creating a bumpy putting surface. To ensure a uniform putting surface, as well as to bring the greens up to the requisite speed, the USGA chose to cut them to a height that deterred growth altogether.

"We've never shaved the greens as close before," Pebble Beach's greenkeeper Roger Larson said. "They are now down to three thirty-seconds of an inch in height instead of the customary three-sixteenths, and that's pretty thin. Some of the grass on the greens has begun to wilt and we're going to have to syringe the greens morning and night to save them."

Three new tees were built, which extended the course by 40 yards, pushing it to 6,815 yards, still short by Open standards. On the par-3 fifth hole, trees were trimmed so that the hole no longer would be called the only dogleg par 3 in golf.

The USGA also narrowed the landing areas in the fairways to 30 yards, miniscule targets that shrunk precipitously when the wind blew and the difficulty of the rough entered a player's mindset and derailed his preshot routine.

Nicklaus called it "a scary golf course, probably the best strategy course in the world."

In one instance, Nicklaus and Arnold Palmer came to the players' defense by voicing their opposition to the narrow landing area on the difficult eighth hole, widely regarded as one of the finest par 4s in the world.

"The blind tee shot to a flat cliff-top plateau," *Golf World* wrote, "gives no inkling of the spectacular right-angled second shot across a gaping oceanic chasm. Depending on the placement of the drive, the shot will range from a three- to a five-iron to a tiny green dwarfed by five large bunkers."

The USGA actually agreed with Palmer and Nicklaus, and on the eve of the tournament extended the width of the fairway by four critical yards on the right side.

"The eighth was unrealistic before," Nicklaus said. "The way it was, the tee shot went from left to right, which put the ball in the rough. The fairway is still narrow, but where the ball caught the rough before, it's now in the fairway. It restores the finest second shot in golf."

Pebble Beach's host professional was Art Bell, who did not venture out onto a limb in predicting that Nicklaus would win the '72 Open. The score he predicted was worth noting, however. "He's played Pebble Beach so well in the past," Bell said of Nicklaus. "He's the type of player who hits the ball high, and is very strong in getting out of the rough. The thing that makes Pebble Beach tough is that the links are not protected by trees. Winds make oceanside courses hard to play. Figuring at least one or two days of westerly winds, which are not real strong winds, I'd say 290 should be in the top three."

Lynnford Lardner Jr., the USGA president, agreed that 290 would be the target in the event the wind blew. "The course," he said, "is a hard and fair test."

Frank Beard, the tour's resident iconoclast, attempted to debunk Pebble Beach's merits as an Open test in his monthly column in *Golf Digest*. He wrote that "the public has been brainwashed" into believing a course is great on the basis of its hosting a U.S. Open. "I keep hearing and reading that [Pebble Beach] is a great course. It has a great tradition, and the area is unbelievably beautiful, but it's not the greatest course we play. Pebble Beach, if it weren't for the usually disastrous weather during the Crosby tournament, would be much more vulnerable. The USGA will have to grow a lot more rough and narrow the fairways, put the pins in tough spots, and hope the weather isn't too good. The USGA says it has selected a great course, but in the next breath says that there will have to be three new tees and a half dozen new bunkers. If it's a great course, you shouldn't have to do all that. I'm not knocking the course—I'm simply stating a philosophy."

He failed to note that for an Open the USGA *always* grows more rough, narrows the fairways, and puts pins in tough spots. As for the construction of three new tees and the addition of six bunkers, this represented little more than cosmetic surgery. Moreover, all courses evolve over time. Augusta National, which Beard called "a great course," undergoes minor alterations virtually every year.

Pebble Beach is inanimate, obviously, and as a result presumably cannot read. Yet it seemingly got its dander up by what Beard wrote; he shot 85 in the first round of the Open there.

The conditions were temperate, too: sunny and warm, with a comforting breeze. Pebble Beach nonetheless demonstrated its mettle. Only six players broke par—Nicklaus, Kermit Zarley, Chi Chi Rodriguez, Orville Moody, Tom Shaw, and Mason Rudolph—and all were tied for the lead with one-under par 71s.

The defending champion was Lee Trevino, who earlier in the week had been hospitalized with pneumonia and was noticeably weakened. "But hell, man, this is like the Indy 500, once a year," he said, "and if the engine blows, get a new one. I've got to give it a try." He gamely toured Pebble Beach in 74 strokes.

The scoring average in the first round was 78, an abysmal number by professional standards. Unlike your local muny on a Saturday morning, the objective at this level ordinarily is not to break 80. Yet a number of quality players failed on that count, including Dave Stockton, Ben Crenshaw (though he was still an amateur), Doug Sanders, Charles Coody, and Al Geiberger.

Jim Jamieson, part of a threesome that shot 82, 85, and 80, jokingly asked a USGA official in the scoring tent, "Can we turn in a best ball?"

Ras Allen was one-under par through seven holes and finished with a fourteen-over par 86. "It's an occupational hazard," he said.

Pebble Beach was dubbed *Double Bogey by the Sea* as a result of its nasty disposition, which to that point of the tournament had largely been kept in check. "I think the course will never play easier this week," said Nicklaus, who expressed surprise at the plethora of high scores.

The weather for the second round was a carbon copy of the first, and so was the scoring, the average improving only a tick, to 77.9.

Beard again was among its victims. On the eighteenth hole of the second round, Beard hit a poor tee shot and a poor second as well. Forced to wait for the group ahead to clear the green, Beard walked to the edge of the short cliff to the left of the fairway and stood staring blankly out to sea. Finally, a lone voice emanated from the gallery. "Don't jump, Frank!" it said. "We know you didn't mean those things you wrote."

A few minutes later, Beard completed play at eighteen, concluding his '72 Open with rounds of 85 and 80, proving that Pebble Beach indeed had enough weapons to defend itself against an Open assault, or at least whatever contributions that Beard intended to make to one.

Rudolph, among the first-round leaders, shot a second-round 80. "This course," he said, "is built around my game. It doesn't touch any part of it."

Nicklaus shot 73 in the second round and retained a share of the lead, again with five other players. "It may be the first time the USGA starts a Monday play-off with a shotgun start," said Bay Area sportswriter Art Spander, noting the logjam.

Arnold Palmer, meanwhile, equaled the day's best round, a 68 that moved him to within a stroke of the lead and titillated the crowd into considering that he might have another major championship in him, eight years removed from his last one. Palmer was playing without his contact lenses, a hedge against the irritation wind causes those wearing contacts. "Besides," he said, "I felt I was familiar enough with the course to recognize distances."

The third round presented yet another difficult challenge, and only one player, Jim Wiechers, bettered 70. Nicklaus finally broke from the pack, shooting an even-par 72 that left him a stroke ahead of Bruce Crampton, Trevino, Kermit Zarley, and Palmer.

An even-par score of 216 leading through three rounds surprised Nicklaus, who failed to recognize the degree to which the wind would be a factor. "If you had told me that earlier, I would have said you were cracked," he said. "It's the wind. I didn't expect this much in June. It's more than we get most of the time in the Crosby."

Whatever lingering doubts existed regarding Pebble Beach's ability to deliver on its promise of a memorable major championship were scattered by the gale-force winds that swept across the Monterey Peninsula on Sunday. The weather was asserting itself in earnest.

The USGA had anticipated overcast skies on Sunday, so it chose not to water the greens on Saturday night, to allow them to firm up. Its forecast proved erroneous, however, and skies were clear, inviting a strong westerly wind on Sunday morning that entirely dried out the greens, rendering them so hard and fast they were nearly unplayable.

The winds were so prohibitive that a regatta scheduled nearby, in a body of water misidentified as Stillwater Cove, was canceled by small-craft warnings. The ubiquitous boats in Carmel Bay also remained moored for the day.

"I can't recall a day like this when we were almost not playing golf," Nicklaus said. "Golfing skills were almost eliminated. Half the greens were dead. They were dried out by the wind and every green had a different speed. I don't think the USGA was looking for this much wind the last day and rolled the greens the night before. If you made a putt it was luck, not skill. All you could do was avoid three-putting. It was just like a seaside course in Britain and I had been expecting something like this all week."

The script needed no editing: A Nicklaus-Palmer duel for the national championship, in a remarkable setting, with the world invited to watch, blow by blow.

ABC Television producer Chuck Howard knew that airing only the last six holes at Pebble Beach would prevent the audience from witnessing the heart and soul of the course, the seaside holes that made the course treacherous, notably six through ten. He had twenty-two cameras with which to work, and began pondering how to propitiously use them. The configuration of Pebble, the aforementioned rudimentary figure eight, in an unusually compact layout, led him to conclude that for the first time in televised golf history, a network could show virtually the entire final round. In this case, ABC could broadcast live from the fifth hole on, with parts of the first four holes shown on tape via handheld cameras.

Nicklaus birdied the par-5 second hole, at which point he had a three-stroke lead on the field. But when he bogeyed the fourth and fifth holes, he and Palmer were tied for the lead momentarily, just as the national television audience began tuning in. This was high drama, as best as golf can deliver it, anyway.

By the time Nicklaus reached the tenth hole, he had deleted much of the drama from the script. He was four strokes up on a faltering Palmer, who was in dire need of divine intervention. The elements had delivered on his behalf in the past here, defending him according to his exalted status as the King. On the fourteenth hole at Pebble Beach in the 1967 Crosby, Palmer was engaged in a tête-à-tête with Nicklaus, when a 3-wood second shot nicked a tree branch and sent the ball caroming out of bounds. That night, the offending tree was felled by a violent storm, its message implicit: Don't mess with the King.

The tenth tee at Pebble is exposed entirely to the elements and the wind was whipping off the water, and Palmer needed assistance if he intended to reenter the fray. Suddenly, a gust of wind caught Nicklaus in mid-swing and blew him off balance, causing him to push his drive onto the beach, the ball plugging in the sand. He took a penalty stroke and a drop near the edge of the cliff, then hit another onto the beach. This time, the ball was playable from the beach. Ultimately, he completed the hole with a double-bogey 6 that reintroduced the drama to the telecast. Palmer now was only two back, though Nicklaus was not yet concerned.

"I simply thought, 'Well, I had made my one big mistake of the round,'" he said. "Everyone else was making at least one like that, maybe more, and so I refused to worry. Another hole like that I would have been a little excited."

On the par-3 twelfth hole, measuring 205 yards, Nicklaus hit what he thought was a perfect 3-iron shot that landed on the asphalt green and skidded off the back. "If I stood there for ten years making the shot I'd never make it any better," he said. "But it ran off the back and I had a very delicate shot back to the hole."

Eventually, he faced an eight-foot par putt at precisely the moment Palmer was standing over a ten-foot birdie putt on the fourteenth hole, a moment frozen in time. Had Nicklaus missed his and Palmer made his, they'd have been tied. ABC went to a split screen to show them both, and they struck their putts virtually in unison. A national TV audience watched, mesmerized, securing Pebble Beach's place in the pantheon of great Open courses, as Nicklaus made his putt and Palmer missed. "That," Nicklaus said, "was the most important putt I made all day."

Palmer played himself out of contention with bogeys at the next two holes and eventually finished third. Nicklaus, meanwhile, was three strokes ahead of Crampton when he arrived at the 218-yard, par-3 seventeenth with a menacingly shallow green, and, to boot, it was playing into the teeth of the wind.

On the eve of the final round, Nicklaus was haunted by a recurring nightmare that caused him a fitful sleep. "I arrived at the seventeenth tee every time with a comfortable three-stroke lead," he said, "but there was no way I could make par there with the cup cut left of the hump in the green. Finally, I decided to take the bogey and go on to eighteen. There, now leading by only two shots, all I could do was hit the tee shot either into the ocean on the left or out of bounds on the right. I tried the driver, then the three-wood, then the one-iron, then went through them all again and either dunked the ball or knocked it OB every time. Finally, I couldn't stand it any longer and leaped out of bed."

"What's wrong, Jack?" his wife, Barbara, asked.

"I've played the seventeenth and eighteenth holes for two hours and I can't play them," he replied. "I don't know what I'm going to do if I get there this afternoon with a three-stroke lead, but I'm sure not going to play them again right now."

He called it the worst dream he's ever had about golf, "just awful," he said.

Yet here he was, standing on the seventeenth tee in the final round of the U.S. Open, with the same three-stroke lead that haunted him the night before.

Golf World magazine described the seventeenth hole this way: "Woods and long irons will be needed to reach the hourglass green lying in a ring of sand at an angle to the line of flight. A humpback links the two surfaces. Beyond the sand, the rocks lie in wait to dispatch an errant shot to a watery grave. This grueling par 3 could be a telling factor."

The wind was gusting and Nicklaus took a one-iron, a club that, Dan Jenkins had written, was virtually impossible from which to squeeze a quality shot, noting they were as rare as an understanding wife. It is among the reasons that one-irons eventually became an endangered species. Nicklaus, of course, was the exception; he had both an understanding wife and the ability to execute a quality one-iron shot, even under pressure.

Nicklaus waggled his club and took one final look at the pin, left of the hump on the seventeenth green, then cocked his head slightly to the right, the trigger that started his swing. In mid-swing, a strong gust of wind hit him, shutting closed the face of the club, requiring that he make a split-second adjustment before impact. Nicklaus nonetheless struck it perfectly—a low, boring shot that sliced through the wind and was headed straight at the flagstick. The ball took one bounce, glanced off the stick, and stopped five inches from the cup, leaving him a tap-in birdie that gave him a four-stroke lead.

It will forever be remembered as one of the two best and most famous one-iron shots ever hit, joining Hogan's one-iron to the eighteenth green in the final round of the Open at Merion in 1950. Nicklaus tapped in for birdie, virtually clinching his third U.S. Open victory. Only a formality remained—the otherwise difficult par-5 eighteenth.

After hitting their tee shots at eighteen, Nicklaus and his playing partner, Lee Trevino, made their way up the fairway and toward the Monterey pine that bisects the fairway, guarding the landing area. A group of protesters—described in one account as "scruffy youngsters"—had padlocked themselves to the tree and had unfurled banners protesting the Vietnam War. The USGA had the banners confiscated, but there was not enough time to cut through the chain that had tethered them to the tree. Officials instructed them to stay as close as they could to the tree, lest they stop a tee shot with their heads.

The USGA might have consulted on the matter with Trevino, a former marine with a low tolerance for anti-establishment youth. Trevino had a ready solution to the dilemma presented by the protesters.

"Put a match to that tree and the key will appear mighty fast," he said to Nicklaus, who only a few shots removed from the thirteenth major championship victory of his career, broke into hearty laughter at Trevino's suggestion.

Nicklaus went on to bogey the eighteenth and still won by three strokes, by shooting a two-over par 74 that, given the circumstances, was among the finest closing rounds of his career.

"Very, very difficult conditions," Nicklaus said many years later. "Very windy. Very dry. Watching everybody just sort of demolish themselves, and I just kept playing golf, kept playing golf. And I played pretty well."

Only Mason Rudolph, with a 70, bettered par, and only amateur Jim Simons equaled par in the final round. Twenty-five players failed to break 80 and the scoring average was 78.8.

Nicklaus's seventy-two hole score was 290 (two over par), the second highest winning Open score since World War II and the number called by the host pro, Art Bell. Only ten players completed seventy-two holes in fewer than 300 strokes.

"It was the first time you had to absolutely plan the perfect shot, shot after shot, then execute the perfect shot, then be lucky," Billy Casper said. "Every round, not just the last."

Aside from the luck factor, this is precisely the challenge the USGA wishes to issue to players expecting to win the U.S. Open.

George Archer demonstrated neither perfect shots nor luck and eventually ran out of patience near the end of a final round in which he shot 87. On the eighteenth tee, Archer deliberately hit his tee shot into Carmel Bay.

Crampton, who finished second, was asked the rhetorical question: whether the course was tough. "Tough?" he answered. "Tough isn't the word. I thought it was impossible. Today, instead of aiming at the green, we were aiming at the golf course."

It may have been tough, but it too was an overwhelming success from any vantage point. Less than six months before the tournament had started, more than 14,000 season tickets had been sold, at an average price of more than thirty-six dollars, erasing all financial concerns.

Even without the brutality of the wind transforming Pebble Beach into an unplayable lie on Sunday, the course withstood the best players in the world taking their best shots.

"If I had only one more round of golf to play, I would play it at Pebble Beach," Nicklaus said some time later. "I can't imagine ever creating a finer all-around test of golf in a more sensational setting."

Of course, winning generally irrigates a love affair with a golf course and causes it to blossom. Nicklaus's victories in the U.S. Amateur and U.S. Open there provided the bond uniting the pair forever. "The words Pebble Beach should be engraved on the heart of Jack Nicklaus," Herbert Warren Wind once wrote.

The best testimonials to Pebble Beach's performance came from those in the British press corps, who were smitten. One even rated Pebble Beach the best seaside links in the world, better even than his own back home, "with only Muirfield a close second," he wrote, "and not very close at that."

After Nicklaus had closed out his victory, he received a phone call from President Nixon, who was especially impressed by the deuce the winner had made on the seventeenth hole, "when the chips were down," Nixon said.

History would go on to show that Nixon failed to perform similarly when the chips were down, as they were at precisely this moment in time. The newspapers the next day obviously featured Nicklaus's victory, which earned him the second leg of the grand slam he was so assiduously pursuing that year. Though no one could have known it at the time, it eventually would prove to be only the second most important story of the day.

On the front page of a newspaper, Dateline Washington, D.C., a story's lead paragraph read: "James McCord, a former CIA agent seized during a weekend break-in at Democratic National Headquarters at Watergate, was hired as a Republican security coordinator on the recommendation of a ranking Secret Service agent."

8

MILLER TIME

OAKMONT COUNTRY CLUB, 1973

Henry C. Fownes may or may not have had dandruff and a navy blue blazer on which to display it, but he was a kindred spirit to those possessing such accoutrements of golf authority. When Fownes, a steel magnate, built Oakmont Country Club in 1904 near the Allegheny River on the outskirts of Pittsburgh, his goal was to have the toughest golf course in the world.

The USGA accordingly loves Oakmont Country Club, recognizing that its heart has always been in the right place, which is to say that it has been stored away in a thimble. This is the generous explanation, anyway; some would say that Oakmont, like the USGA, has no heart at all.

This might be why Oakmont and the USGA are so compatible

and why the latter keeps returning the Open to Oakmont, this and the fact that it ranks among the great golf courses in the world. The USGA has taken the Open to Oakmont seven times, equaling Baltusrol Golf Club in Springfield, New Jersey, for hosting a record number of Opens.

Oakmont is a mean, nasty golf course, even as the members play it, or, should we say, *especially* as the members play it. The course, Johnny Miller said, is always Open-ready, even in the intervening years. "This course and Shinnecock Hills are probably more Open-ready, day in and day out, than any other," he said. Indeed, Oakmont is said to have the only greens that the USGA is required to slow down in setting the course up for the U.S. Open. This is a point of pride to the members, who will politely agree that Oakmont, as it plays for the U.S. Open, is difficult. Yet they will invariably add, "But if you really want to see it tough, come play the member-guest."

Fownes and his son, William C., were autocratic rulers who always informed their superintendents to listen politely to the USGA, then do not do as it says, but do as they say. And what they usually said was to go out to the course at four o'clock in the morning, under the cover of darkness, long before the USGA officials arrived, and take the club's renowned 750 pound roller, and roll the greens to ensure that they play as hard and fast as an ice rink and uphold the integrity of the course.

Henry Fownes's philosophy was that "a shot poorly played should be a shot irrevocably lost." Moreover, Oakmont was designed to place a premium on every shot; there are no breathers, not a single hole that would permit the golfer to let down his guard for a moment, without bringing a high number into play. Fownes felt it was the least a course could do, to demand a tournament winner use care and caution in the execution of every shot.

William C. Fownes became Oakmont's chairman-of-the-greens committee in 1911 and later a caretaker of his father's wishes to ensure that Oakmont was the toughest course in the world. When William watched golfers play the course, he would note when one struck a poor shot that went unpunished, then would instruct his greenkeeper to install another bunker that might have prevented this kind of transgression.

One weekend, a few months prior to the 1935 U.S. Open at Oakmont, W. C. was out of town, when a stalwart of a man carried a fairway bunker from the seventh tee, a shot of more than 240 yards in the air. Emil Loeffler, his trusted greenkeeper, noted it and, according to his instructions when such ignominy was done to the course, phoned W. C. to inform him. When Fownes returned on Monday, he carefully studied the situation, then instructed Loeffler to install a small bunker just beyond the one that had been carried.

At one time, more than 350 bunkers had been installed, which surely created the most felicitous meeting of land and sand in the golf universe, as Robert Louis Stevenson might have written. This represented an average of more than nineteen bunkers per hole. Only 180 of them remain, still a notable number, and one of them is among the most infamous in the world, the *Church Pews* bunker between the third and fourth fairways. This is a long, massive stretch of sand that contains eight fingers of grass within it, creating the impression of pews in a church. It is there to snatch errant tee shots on both the third and fourth holes, and is a debilitating place from which to play a second shot in either direction.

"Oakmont," Robert Trent Jones wrote, "is considered one of the world's hardest and most penal courses, and its almost two hundred bunkers are certainly one of the main reasons."

Grantland Rice could have been thinking of Oakmont when he wrote: "The United States Open is the Death Valley of Sportdom. There are gold mines in it, but most of the world's greatest golfers get lost in the sand."

When Henry Fownes built the course, he wanted to replicate a Scottish links course, a curious goal, given the three-hundred miles of land between the property and the nearest sea. To lend his course at least an air of Scottish authenticity, he wanted to install a series of pot bunkers. He was unable to do so because of the inadequate subsurface drainage in the clay on which Oakmont was built. The bunkers had to be shallow, diminishing their severity. To compensate, he had the bunkers dragged with a rake that had long, thick tines, creating deep furrows from which it was nearly impossible to escape without sustaining damage to one's round. Only Willie Turnesa, in fact, mastered the furrows, getting up and down on fourteen of sixteen occasions in the thirty-six-hole final of the U.S. Amateur he won there in 1938, earning him the moniker Willie the Wedge.

The club no longer furrows its bunkers and hasn't since the late '50s, though given its druthers, it would recommence the practice on those occasions when the USGA returns. Given the USGA's ruthless disposition, it is a wonder that the furrows are not resurrected for Open play there.

The bunkers, notably the Church Pews, give Oakmont its most visibly distinguishing characteristic, but its preeminent menace is its greens. They are contoured in a way that they resemble a foreign language to the players, virtually impossible for them to read. Jack Nicklaus surveyed a thirty-five footer in the first round in 1973 and failed to note a small crown until after he had stroked his putt. "I ended up fifteen feet left," he said.

Many of the greens slope from front to back—contrary to most greens elsewhere, which slope back to front—creating something of a backboard to help stop approach shots. And, too, they are perpetually fast, no matter who is playing them—members, guests, or an Open field. The short downhill putt that misses the cup frequently leaves the player with a long uphill putt coming back.

"Oakmont," Sal Johnson wrote in his book, *The Official U.S. Open Almanac*, "may be the quintessential U.S. Open course." The USGA's ecstasy with Oakmont is that the agony was built in. The architect Robert Trent Jones called it "an ugly beauty."

Gene Sarazen won the PGA Championship there in 1922, yet

paid tribute to its brutality. "Oakmont," he said, "has the charm of a punch to the head."

Oakmont has fulfilled its obligation to the USGA by routinely identifying the best player, reflected in the history that abounds there. It was at Oakmont in the 1962 Open that a portly twenty-two-year-old upended the King. When Nicklaus defeated Arnold Palmer in a play-off, it altered the course of golf history, to the chagrin of Arnie's Army, which initially hated Nicklaus as a result. Sarazen, Bobby Jones, Tommy Armour, Sam Snead, and Ben Hogan have won major championships there as well.

For the 1973 Open at Oakmont, the USGA had lofty expectations, which it typically defined as a winning score over par. In four previous Opens at Oakmont, the only players to finish seventy-two holes under par were Hogan, Nicklaus, and Palmer, a trio as gilded as any in golf history, and at that, each of them only shot one-under par 283.

The bunkers are the course's first line of defense, the greens its last line. "These are the fastest greens I've ever played on and I've been playing golf for twenty-seven years," Raymond Floyd said.

Sam Snead said he once marked his ball with a dime at Oakmont, "but when I came back to put my ball down I realized that the dime had slid two feet." He was kidding. Apparently.

Lloyd Mangrum won the '46 Open at Oakmont and said that putting its greens "is like putting down a marble staircase and trying to stop the ball halfway down."

"Any time you two-putt at Oakmont you're passing somebody up," Lee Trevino said.

Dave Stockton was among the finest putters of his or any other generation, and even he lamented having to putt on Oakmont's greens. "You have to lag your lag putts," he said. "Nobody likes to putt scared, but you have to putt scared on these greens."

This was the backdrop on the eve of the 1973 U.S. Open at Oakmont. A *New York Times* headline on a story advancing the tournament read, PUTTING KEY TO U.S. OPEN. The piece addressed Nicklaus's bid for a fourteenth major championship, which would exceed Bobby Jones's record of 13 majors. Whoever won, the story concluded, "may depend on how well they putt and judge the speed of Oakmont's famed putting surfaces."

For once, the USGA escaped criticism for the way the course was set up. The fairways provided ample room, by Open standards, and the rough was not of a height in which players might get lost for days. "They would eat this course alive if it weren't for the greens," Trevino said on the eve of the tournament. "I've never putted greens this fast."

Gary Player, the perennial Open optimist who never encountered a difficult course that he regarded as unfair, opened the tournament with a four-under par 67 that gave him a three-stroke lead. "By Sunday, I think you will realize what a good round it was," he said.

Maybe, maybe not.

The greens performed to Oakmont's demanding standards. Charlie Sifford took so many putts on the seventh green that he lost count. "I didn't five-putt because of the green," he said. "I five-putted because I didn't give a damn." In fact, he six-putted.

Player again bettered par in the second round, with a 70, and retained his lead, this time one shot over Jim Colbert. An alternate, Long Island club professional Gene Borek, emerged from obscurity with a six-under par 65, the best round ever shot at Oakmont. Borek, incidentally, had gotten into the tournament when Dave Hill assessed the difficulty of the course and measured it against the state of his game and decided to withdraw four holes into his first practice round. "I couldn't make the cut here if I had a free throw on every hole," Hill said, typically blunt, but avoiding the mean-spirited criticism that tangled him in controversy at the '70 Open at Hazeltine.

Borek's round deserved a hearty round of applause, followed by an investigation into how Oakmont allowed an unknown club pro to break the course record and to have done so in the U.S. Open. He was not the only perpetrator; an Open-record nineteen players broke par.

USGA Executive Director P. J. Boatwright explained that the greens had been watered the night before as a hedge against warmer temperatures baking them out. "We wanted to keep them firm," he said, "but we were afraid they would get as hard as bricks and that's why they were watered down."

The truth may have been watered down as well. *The New York Times* reported Boatwright as saying that the greens had only been doused for five minutes. The *Los Angeles Times* reported that the sprinklers apparently had been left running longer than ordered and that Boatwright acknowledged that the greens were wetter than they were supposed to have been.

"You could see water around your shoes," Palmer said.

The truth, the USGA's Sandy Tatum acknowledged twenty-eight years later, was that "the sprinkler system either malfunctioned or was improperly set. To be charitable, we'll say it malfunctioned. But it went on all night. When I went out early in the morning, the golf course was virtually under water. It had been tremendously over-watered. The reaction was wonderful. The place was in a state of shock. The superintendent couldn't handle it. He took the position that we had ordered him to do it. That was a blatant prevarication."

The greens were not as treacherous as the USGA or the membership at Oakmont preferred them to be; the water had softened them to a point that they were far more receptive to holding approach shots and slowed them down moderately, diminishing the hazard of putting on them. It was reflected in the scoring; the scoring average of 75.4 was two-and-a-half shots better than it had been for the second round at Pebble Beach a year earlier.

"The course couldn't be better," Palmer said, speaking on behalf of a field of players who recognized that the overwatering was akin to Oakmont having had its teeth pulled. It had lost its bite. "Conditions were perfect," Palmer said.

Nicklaus was a lone dissenter, for selfish reasons to which he admitted. The harder a course, the better his chances of prevailing. "I like [the greens] as hard and fast as this table," he said, rapping the hardwood. "Not many guys can handle them like that."

Rain on the morning of the third round prevented the greens from drying out and again kept Oakmont in check. "As the sun broke through," *The New York Times* wrote, "the putting surfaces were slower than the speedy glasslike greens the officials had hoped for and that Nicklaus likes."

Nicklaus was four strokes behind a foursome tied for the lead— Palmer, Julius Boros, Jerry Heard, and John Schlee, each of them three-under par. Schlee was an astrology devotee who attributed his exalted standing to "Mars [being] in conjunction with my natal moon."

How that reconciled with his first shot of the final round was never explained. Schlee sliced his ball into a hedge, right of the first fairway, an unplayable lie that led to a double-bogey, ultimately costing him the championship. Of course, he was paired with Palmer, a Latrobe, Pennsylvania, native, for whom playing at Oakmont was virtually a home game, with a spirited home-crowd advantage. "Being paired with Palmer," Schlee said, "is like a two-stroke penalty."

Johnny Miller, meanwhile, stood 6 shots in arrears of the leaders and was tied for 13th when the final round began. He was paired with Miller Barber and went off at 1:36 P.M., nearly an hour before the leaders.

He began his round with four straight birdies and birdied four holes in a five-hole stretch on the back nine, en route to shooting an Open-record 63, eight-under par. He finished the tournament at five-under par 279, leading at the time by a stroke. He then sat and waited to see whether anyone would derail the express train he had taken to the winner's circle.

"If there was ever a round that I played that felt like somebody helped me from above," said Miller, a devout Mormon, "this was it." Prior to the round, he said he heard a voice, "clear as a bell," telling him to open his stance. "I opened it up and I hit every green," he said.

Palmer's bid was undone in part by the shock he encountered when he saw Miller's name ahead of his on the leaderboard, as well as the score that Miller shot. Palmer still had seven holes to play. He immediately bogeyed three straight holes to fall from contention.

"After all the golf I've played," Palmer said to his playing partner, Schlee, as they made their way up the eighteenth fairway, "I shouldn't have been that shocked when I saw the scoreboard."

No one would catch Miller, who became the Open champion with what arguably could be called the finest round in Open history. Statistics state his case for him. He hit every green in regulation and on ten occasions put his ball inside fifteen feet, and on five occasions, six feet or closer. He reckoned his average first putt measured no more than ten feet.

Those arguing against him noted the overnight rain that had further softened the course, making it vulnerable. Tatum argues that the course was vulnerable from the moment the sprinklers malfunctioned. "There is an element there," he said, "and I don't want to detract from what I consider one of the greatest performances in the history of the game, but . . . the golf course never recovered."

Oakmont in effect failed to adequately protect itself, and Miller and others delivered a knockout punch that the USGA had expected to throw itself, with its bunker overload and table-top greens. This time, those in the navy blue blazers were bloodied and bowed and ostensibly pining for revenge.

When darkness had descended on Oakmont, its head professional, Lew Worsham, was walking the premises and reflecting on Miller's 63 and what the club's founder, Henry Fownes, would have made of such an assault on his course. The thought occurred to Worsham that Henry was rolling over in his grave.

"Lie still, Mr. Fownes," Worsham was said to have muttered. "Lie still."

9

PAYBACK

Winged Foot Golf Club, as the story goes, once included a man notorious among the membership for his inability to begin a round with an agreeable effort from the first tee. Invariably, David Mulligan would re-tee and hit another, a shot his friends took to calling a Mulligan.

Still smarting from Johnny Miller's final-round rebuke at Oakmont Country Club a year earlier, the USGA may have wanted its own mulligan and had come to the right place, Winged Foot Golf Club in Mamaroneck, New York, in the suburbs thirty minutes north of New York City, on the grounds on which the mulligan entered the lexicon in 1937.

Miller's unforgettable final round from the perspective of history was a regrettable one from the vantage point of those given the charge of ensuring that Open courses don't yield so passively to the manifold skills of the modern golfer. The West Course at Winged Foot Golf Club, in the hands of a vengeful USGA, was a suitable hedge against it happening twice.

Both the West Course and the East Course at Winged Foot were built by Albert Warren Tillinghast, an architectural giant about whom the eminent author Dick Schaap wrote:

> *A proper Philadelphian by birth, an improper Philadelphian by incli-*
> *nation, Tillie was an heroic drinker, an habitual gambler, a dapper*
> *dresser, a golfer skilled enough to finish twenty-fifth in the 1910*
> *U.S. Open, a phrasemaker clever enough to invent the term*
> *"birdie," a misguided investor in Broadway musicals, the operator*
> *of perhaps the world's only combination speakeasy and golf club—*
> *and an acquaintance of Trotsky's. He was also one of the great*
> *architects of American Golf.*

Tillinghast was a ruffian (once known as Tillie the Terror) turned bon vivant, who fell into design when at thirty-two he was asked to build a course. From the outset, Tillinghast excelled at course design. He would oversee construction from the seat of a shooting stick, shouting instructions between pulls from his hip flask. Among his best work was Baltusrol Golf Club and the Black Course at Bethpage State Park Golf Course, each of them future Open sites, as well as Winged Foot.

When Tillinghast was hired to design Winged Foot, his instructions were to build a man-sized golf course. "As the various holes came to life," Tillie once wrote of the West Course, "they were of a sturdy breed. The holes are like men, all rather similar from foot to neck, but with the green showing the same varying characters as human faces. The contouring of the greens places great premium on the placement of the drives, but never is there the necessity of facing a prodigious carry of the sink-or-swim sort. It is only in the knowledge that the next shot must be played with rifle accuracy that brings the realization that the drive must be placed."

Of course, Oakmont Country Club was no pitch-and-putt, either, yet it had meekly surrendered to Johnny Miller's precision a year before. Just in case man-sized no longer was sufficient to thwart the best players in the game, the USGA chose to provide Winged Foot the means necessary to repel them, and it was evident from the moment the players stepped onto the course.

"They probed the 6,961-yard, par-70 layout for weaknesses and found none," *The New York Times* reported in the aftermath of a practice round there. Winged Foot's most prohibitive characteristic was the hard, fast, contoured greens that placed a premium on leaving the ball beneath the hole. The downhill putt that missed the hole had nothing to slow its momentum. "The downhill putts," the *Times* added, "are not perilous, they are suicidal."

Sandy Tatum was the USGA's chairman of the championship committee and the man on whom the responsibility fell to set up Winged Foot for the Open. On the eve of the tournament, it was his contention that the greens were perfect. "They have been cut to nine sixty-fourths of an inch," he said. "They are reacting exactly as we would like. We can cut them another one sixty-fourth, but we probably won't."

The greens made the golf course, according to Jack Nicklaus. "They're the most severely undulating greens I've seen in the Open since we were here last time."

The severe slopes effectively diminished the size of the greens, by shrinking the actual target. Placing your ball on the wrong side of the slope was akin to missing the green, and required a deft touch to save par.

Ben Hogan once likened the tee shot to one of these hazardous greens, the 190-yard, par-3 tenth, to "hitting a three-iron into some guy's bedroom." It was indeed a small window through which to hit a large shot.

When Billy Casper won the Open at Winged Foot in 1959, he actually laid up short of the green and the trouble protecting it on the par 3s, then attempted to rely on his short game to save par.

Casper was a two-time Open champion and among the best putters in golf, yet he considered himself lost on Winged Foot's greens and called the course the toughest he'd ever seen in an Open. "You have no control over the ball on the greens," he said. "No feel. You just hit and watch it wander around. And the course is so long you're always hitting a two-iron or a four-wood on your second shot. I believe you should use every club in your bag in an Open, but the USGA believes in long irons, not middle or short irons."

The rough in 1974 was typically penal. "The grass in this rough is young and soft," Sam Snead said. "It isn't dead and the ball doesn't sit up for you. It just drops to the bottom and you have to dig it out."

The fairways were thirty yards wide and framed by the rough and trees. Missing the fairway lengthened the odds of finding the green with the next shot, and those that missed were subjected to either more rough or possibly a shot from a bunker eight feet deep.

The bunkers were debilitating in their own right, a fitting complement to the difficult greens, a double-barrel assault. Fred Corcoran, a Winged Foot member and a former manager of the PGA Tour, said, "The fellow who gets in a lot of bunkers and gets up and down in two all the time will be playing with a prayer book in his pocket."

In summary, Bobby Nichols said that Winged Foot "looks to me like eighteen bogeys." Tillinghast and the USGA had conspired to produce a course that Gary Player said "will shake you into the ground."

"Perhaps," Schaap wrote, "if A. W. Tillinghast had designed the Alamo, and the USGA had toughened it up, the Mexican siege would have failed."

Frank Hannigan recalled that Tatum and P. J. Boatwright, the two men ultimately responsible for the setup, had played a round at Winged Foot that spring. Tatum was an exceptional amateur golfer, a former club champion at the Olympic Club and participant in the U.S.

Amateur. "Sandy shot a ridiculously low score that day, a miracle round, and said that the course wasn't very hard," Hannigan said.

The suggestion, denied by Tatum, was that he had gauged the difficulty of the course by the ease with which he handled it and deduced that it needed an injection of gristle.

When June and the Open arrived, Winged Foot was angry and the membership knew it. One rumor circulating through the premises was that the members had wagered more than $100,000 that the winning score would be even-par 280 or higher. Billy Casper was a devout Mormon and not a betting man, but he was astute enough to recognize illogical odds when he encountered them, and he was certain he had done so with this over-under line. "Two-eighty might win by 10 shots," said Casper, who shot 282 in winning by a stroke in 1959.

Dave Hill suggested that even conceding a player each green in regulation and placing the ball twenty feet from the hole still would not enable him to break 280.

The players' reaction (or overreaction, as was often suspected) seemed to be typical Open posturing. Only a year before, the members at Oakmont were said to have had a similar amount of money wagered on a winning score of 280 or higher and lost when Miller closed with a 63 and finished at 279.

Frank Beard usually found a way to be heard above the din and did so again in a *Golf Digest* column in which he opined on the USGA's motivation. "The USGA feels the Open is the only event on the tour run by amateurs and by golly these hot-shot pros aren't going to come in and stomp all over their championship and their golf course," he wrote. "These are the best players in the world and you're telling me they shouldn't break par? Nonsense. I can take any course in the world and trick it up so nobody can break 100, but the object isn't to keep the scores as high as possible. It's almost as if the Open has boiled down to a contest between the pros and the USGA."

In a Wednesday news conference, on the eve of the first round, Sandy Tatum denied that Winged Foot was set up to extract revenge for Miller's 63 the year before. "No," he said, "we were not concerned with Miller's unbelievably great score. Six of the greatest players in the world—Jack Nicklaus, Arnold Palmer, Lee Trevino, Tom Weiskopf, Gary Player, and Julius Boros—were in contention that day and only one, Nicklaus, broke 70."

Tatum then defended the course setup and the USGA's intentions. "The USGA policy," he said, "is not to confound the best players, but to find out who they are. We look for a course that will force them to bring all their skills to bear. Winged Foot does that. It requires two qualities: head and heart."

Over time, Tatum's defense of the Winged Foot setup was chiseled and sanded and generally refined, until he was alleged to have said for posterity, "Our intention is not to embarrass the greatest players in the world, but to identify them."

On Wednesday morning, a few light sprinkles began teasing the players, who collectively might have done a rain dance had they known one. They were rooting for a downpour to soften the greens and eliminate at least a modicum of the quandary from them. One player mused that if it did begin to pour, the USGA would cover the greens with tarps to keep them dry.

John Schlee, the tour's resident astrologer, was reading the stars through the clouds hovering over Winged Foot. A year earlier, Schlee had credited his fine play to "Mars [being] in conjunction with my natal moon." He finished second to Miller, losing by a stroke. On the eve of the '74 Open, he was asked what the stars held for him this time around. "I'm a Capricorn," he said somewhat morosely.

And?

"Richard Nixon is a Capricorn," Schlee replied, as the president's problems were building toward his imminent resignation.

Johnny Miller, the defending champion and among the more candid players in golf, as the NBC golf audience would learn years later, was holding forth in the press tent and discussing Open setups and how they narrow the list of contenders. "There's a field of a hundred-and-fifty here, but only twenty-five who can really play this course," he said, "and you know how good they are because they're the same names year after year. The others wander around in a daze, saying, 'What am I doing here?' "

Miller also noted that great imagination was necessary to putt the Winged Foot greens. "You have to imagine what the putt is going to do," he said. "It's going to be a joke watching a mediocre putter putt."

Jack Nicklaus in his prime, as he was in 1974, never approached mediocrity on the putting green, yet the first putt he had in earnest at Winged Foot was an ominous one for the field. He was twenty-five feet from the hole for birdie. His putt missed the target, but not the slope on the other side of it, the ball gathering momentum and eventually stopping twenty-eight feet away. His birdie putt was shorter than his par putt. "What an embarrassing way to start the Open," he said.

Nicklaus in fact opened with 4 straight bogeys, news of which led Miller to conclude that "he must have been charmed." Nicklaus played the final fourteen holes in one over par to shoot a 75, trailing leader Gary Player by five strokes. His playing partner, Hubert Green, shot an 81.

"I would hate to see our best-ball," Green said to Nicklaus.

"I would hate to see our worst-ball," Nicklaus replied.

Only Player equaled par; the other 148 players were over par. Player routinely provided the contrary view of an Open setup, applauding virtually all of them, even Winged Foot, perhaps giving him a psychological advantage over those who detested the layouts. "This is how golf should be played," Player said. "No one should be permitted to hit a three-iron iron from the rough. When you miss a putt you pay a penalty. It should be the same with a bad drive. You should be penalized. There's no way you should be rewarded with a birdie after a bad drive."

The scoring average for the first round was 77.8, exactly one stroke higher than it had been the year before, but given that Oakmont played to a par 71 and Winged Foot to a par of 70, the difference was, per player, a full 2 strokes to par.

The grumbling started from the moment the first group finished, and had reached a crescendo by the time the final group walked away from the eighteenth green. The jury was in and the verdict was nearly unanimous: The USGA was guilty of a crime against decency. Whatever its sentence, the jury decreed, it ought to reflect the cruel and unusual punishment that it dispensed.

After completing his first round, Miller came into the press tent and vented. "It's ridiculous," he said. "You hit a perfect drive and you still have to pull out a two-iron to get on. The USGA could not have made the course any harder. This was the Sunday setup, and it's only Thursday. The holes that were with the wind had the pins up front, so there was no green to work with. The holes into the wind had the pins all the way back, making them play thirty yards longer."

"The course makes you feel like a dog," he added, "and the best way to play it is in a fog."

The consensus conclusion was that Miller had betrayed the USGA the year before, and that the organization was determined to seek revenge. It was payback time.

"That was a perfectly understandable assumption," Tatum said more than a quarter-century later, "but it wasn't true. There's one guy in the whole country who could verify without any ifs, ands, or buts, that that wasn't true and you're talking to him."

No one was convinced, least of all the players.

Lee Trevino: "The damn USGA's mad at us for what we did to Oakmont last year. We burnt that one because it rained. Made the greens hold. They ain't taking no chances this time. They got the grass here too damn high."

Larry Ziegler: "Damn him [Miller]. He got the 63 and we're all paying for it."

Miller: "When I walked into the clubhouse, five guys said to me, 'If it hadn't been for you, Miller, it wouldn't have been so hard out there today.' "

"Miller," Dick Schaap wrote in his book on the '74 Open, *Massacre at Winged Foot*, "committed an unpardonable sin in 1973. With his 63 at Oakmont, he shamed the United States Golf Association, which does not believe in scores more than 2 or 3 strokes below par. As a direct result of Miller's transgression, many of his fellow pros fully believe, the USGA decided to transform Winged Foot from a menace into a monster."

The international media corps continued to demand answers and put their questions to Tatum, an attorney by trade, (Stanford and Oxford educated), and capable of holding his own in any debate, even as he was forced to play defense. "The way it unfolded, you'd have thought an atom bomb had been dropped on the place," Tatum said years later.

Golfers on the wrong side of a disturbing day at the office largely are an ill-humored group, yet in the face of U.S. Open adversity, they attempted to mask their anger in humor.

"Putting on those greens is like playing miniature golf without the boards," said Hale Irwin, who opened with a three-over par 73.

"I haven't been this happy since I was in the army," said Rives McBee, his ledger showing an 80.

Homero Blancas repaired to the putting green to work on his downhill putts; by missing a pocketful of them, he had shot a 77. He was asked whether he had any uphill putts in his round. "Sure," he replied. "After each of my downhill putts." It began on the first hole for Blancas, who had a twelve-foot first putt and a twenty-five-foot second putt.

On the tenth hole, Jerry Heard had a fifty-foot downhill par putt that he tapped only with enough force to start the ball rolling. Heard then casually walked toward the hole, eventually arriving there just before the ball trickled into the cup.

John Mahaffey announced that he intended to buy a large pane of glass to take to his room to give him an appropriate surface on which to practice his putting. "If I can make the ball stop going downhill on a pane of glass," he said, "then maybe I can putt these Winged Foot greens."

The greens bore the brunt of the players' criticism, but the rough contributed to the collective misery. Lanny Wadkins hit a shot into the deep rough and ventured in after it. "It can't be too bad a lie," his playing partner Hubert Green yelled over to him. "I can see your knees."

"Once they start hiding the pins," Nicklaus said half-jokingly, "the course will really get tough."

Late Thursday night or early Friday morning, a car was driven across the first green, leaving tire tracks on one of Winged Foot's most difficult greens to putt. A USGA official, Kenneth Gordon, concluded that the culprit was "someone probably drunk who went in the wrong direction leaving the adjacent parking lot."

The damage was minimized by the greenkeeper and was barely discernible once the first group went out for the second round the following morning. "Maybe," Gordon said, smiling, "everyone should really be quite happy that these greens are as hard and fast and automobile-resistant as they are."

When Dave Stockton strode onto the first green that morning, he asked Lee Trevino whether he could see any tire tracks. Trevino said no.

"That gives you an idea how tough these greens are," Stockton said. "Somebody must have mistaken that first one for one of the roads leading to the golf course."

The best round of the day—indeed the tournament—was a 67 shot by Hubert Green, who, on the basis of his 81 in the opening round, had made plane reservations out of town, certain that he would miss the cut. He, too, had worn his trademark Sunday outfit—green from head to toe—since by his estimation he would not be needing it on Sunday. Suddenly, he was tied for nineteenth, only 5 strokes off the lead, with a thirty-six-hole score of 148.

The second round did not produce appreciably better golf, though the scoring average did fall to 77.0. Four players broke par and another four equaled it. The cut was 153, thirteen-over par, the highest cut in relation to par since the '58 Open at Southern Hills.

Emerging as tied for the lead was a gilded group that included Arnold Palmer, Raymond Floyd, Gary Player, and an intruder, Hale Irwin, who had won only two PGA Tour events to that point. Each of them had completed thirty-six holes in three-over par 143.

"GODS OF GOLF" STUMBLE TO MORTALITY, AND GALLERY LOVES IT, read a headline in *The New York Times*. The first paragraph to the story read, " 'I love to see these guys take a beating,' a weekend golfer named Nick Quinn said today at the United States Open. 'You can identify with them.' "

Another paragraph read, " 'It's unreal,' said Bruce Albert, a five-handicap golfer from North Bellmore, Long Island. 'These guys must be embarrassed. They're walking off the greens disgusted. They're behaving like average golfers.' "

This was yet further testimony on behalf of the masses, and the notion that they enjoy watching professional golfers in a debilitating predicament, contrary to the typical pro's position that fans would rather see them having their way with a golf course.

Even ABC Sports producer Chuck Howard weighed in with an opinion in support of the infernal double-bogey. "The guy at home who has to fight for every par he gets doesn't mind seeing the pros in trouble," Howard said. "He's been in bunkers all his life himself. He knows what it's like to struggle."

Winged Foot represented an endurance test, start to finish. "Are these," San Francisco sports writer Art Spander asked Nicklaus, "the best finishing holes you've seen anywhere?"

"Yeah," Nicklaus replied. "The last eighteen of them are very difficult."

Canadian George Knudson was asked to identify the tough holes. "Well, the first three," he said, "the last three, and the twelve in between."

The USGA continued to deflect accusations that it had tricked up the course in an effort to punish the players. "These greens are hard," said Gordon, secretary of the USGA. "There is no really easy placement on any of the greens because they all roll. We're not out to embarrass these golfers. The U.S. Open is the greatest golf course in the world, and we're looking for the greatest golfer in the world.

"Some of the golfers think the pins are set by a bunch of one-hundred hackers who are sadistic. Frank Tatum is a one-handicap from Cypress Point in California and Harry Easterley is a two-handicap from the Country Club of Virginia. We're not tricking up a golf course. Winged Foot is a fine course that needs no tricking up."

Gordon explained the USGA's method for establishing pin placements. Each green is divided into quadrants and assigned a number representing its putting difficulty, one for most severe to four representing the easiest. On any given day, the USGA attempts to have the numbers add to 45, "to keep the degree of difficulty as uniform as we possibly can for the four rounds of the Open," Gordon said. They added to 47 for the first round, 46 for the second round.

The USGA also attempts to cut the hole in a position with a level six-foot radius. The inherent problem in doing so at Winged Foot was the myriad slopes.

"If we don't get some rain," Julius Boros said, lamenting the speed of the greens, "this is going to be a hockey match Saturday and Sunday."

Early on the morning of the third round, after setting the pins at Winged Foot, Tatum, somewhat disheveled as a result of the hour and the job required of him, was returning to the hotel at which he was staying and encountered four players walking toward him.

"Damn, Sandy, you look tired," one of them said.

"You'd look tired, too," another of them said, "if you'd been out all night on your hands and knees waxing the greens."

The carnage continued on Saturday, when only two players shot par or better. One of them was Tom Watson, who had a one-under par 69 to take a one-stroke lead over Hale Irwin, with Palmer 3 strokes behind.

The other 69 was delivered by Jim Colbert, though it included a bogey five at the last hole, when he missed the green with his second shot. "I knew I was in trouble," Colbert said, "when I found those USGA guys on their knees trying to spot the ball for me."

Once the ball was located, Colbert addressed it, then lifted his head to locate the pin. "I glanced up and I absolutely lost sight of the ball," he said. "Then I swung that sand wedge as hard as I could. Whoosh. The sound of the swing was the only sound I heard. I never heard the clubhead hit the ball. That's how strong that grass is."

Nicklaus's putting woes continued, meanwhile, contributing to his round of six-over par 76, leaving him twelve shots from the lead. "I have no problems with the course," he said. "All my problems are with myself. I took 34 putts today and brought my average down. It's gotten to the point where it's a little ridiculous."

The greens at Winged Foot will do that to a man, even the defending champion, already a three-time Open winner whose immortality was impending.

Irwin had another respectable round, a 71, but bemoaned his putting, too. "My touch was not good," he said. "Every time I hit the green I had a crazy putt, over a valley or down a hill. These greens are so fast that once the ball leaves the blade you never know what's going to happen to it."

Three days of perfect weather gave way to a light rain on the morning of the final round, moderately diminishing the fright factor of Winged Foot's greens. Still, they put up a respectable defense. "They were still fast," Irwin said, "but when you putted up a slope the ball stayed there. It didn't come back."

Irwin was a confident young man who wore glasses, a professorial look that belied the fortitude on which he was able to lean under pressure. When he faced a combative course, he refused to back down, a product perhaps of his football training. Irwin was a reasonably good defensive back for the University of Colorado, though a career in professional football was never a viable option, particularly once he began filling out a questionnaire he received from the St. Louis Cardinals. "When I came to the one about how fast I was," Irwin said, "I threw it away."

Speed is a wasted asset in golf, which is a race only in the sense that reaching the finishing line in the fewest number of strokes is the objective. Open courses present obstacles and Irwin was adept at avoiding them, perhaps the result in part of the appreciation he had for difficult tests. "There is no such thing as an easy hole in an Open championship," he said. "A less-than-good shot will lead to a bogey unless it is countered with a better-than-good shot. It brings par the value it should have." In retrospect, he possessed the requisite mind-set to win U.S. Opens.

Three weeks prior to the Open at Winged Foot, Irwin had dreamed that he won the tournament. Asked how he won it, he replied, "On the last hole with two putts from twenty feet."

Two putts from twenty feet is easier to negotiate in a dream than it is in a nightmare, which Winged Foot had represented to the players in 1974. When Irwin arrived at the seventy-second and last green of the Open, he had a cushion for which the dream failed to account—3 putts from twenty feet to win. He needed only 2 of them and won by 2 strokes, a dream come true.

For the rest of the field, the week had been a bad dream, one that came with a title attached, for posterity, *The Massacre at Winged Foot*. The course repelled the best golfers in the world, absolving the USGA of its failings at Oakmont a year earlier. Egos routinely were treated for contusions and the USGA was euphoric.

"An absolute classic," Frank Hannigan called it many years later, "and the hardest golf course in the history of the world. Seven over par in nice weather."

Irwin's seventy-two-hole score was seven-over-par 287, the highest winning score to par since Julius Boros won the '63 Open at nine-over. More important, from the USGA's perspective, it was 12 shots to par higher than Miller's winning score of five-under the year before.

It seldom happens that a tournament, even one as difficult as the U.S. Open, is won by a player who fails to record at least one sub-par round. Irwin's best round of the four was an even-par 70 in the second round. He closed with a three-over par 73, ten shots higher than the winner had shot in the final round a year earlier.

The scoring average at Winged Foot was 76.99 and 412 over-par rounds were played, equaling the number recorded at Oakland Hills in 1951 and only 2 fewer than were shot at the Olympic Club in 1955. Each of those Opens had more players in the field, too. *Golf's Little Big Horn* was among the appellations the '74 Open received.

"The severity of the golf course was almost too much," Irwin said years later. "What a difficult setup we had. It wasn't impossible, but it was extremely difficult. Anything close to par, on any hole, was a very good score."

Even with a man who at the time was an unheralded winner, this Open took its place alongside the more memorable Opens in history, a man-sized course out-muscling the players, a monster they were wholly incapable of bringing to its knees.

"That was the benchmark," Irwin said many years later. "The mother of all golf courses."

The victory was only the third of Irwin's PGA Tour career. But he would go on to win seventeen more times, including two more U.S. Opens, reaffirming to Tatum that the victory at Winged Foot was not a fluke and that he had been justified in setting the course up the way he had.

"It's nice to be able to look back on it and say, I wouldn't change a blade of grass," Tatum said. "That was close to the quintessential Open."

10

TWO-CHIP CHEN

OAKLAND HILLS COUNTRY CLUB, 1985

John Shippen is little more than a footnote to golf history, less than the chapter or, indeed, the book that he probably deserves. He was an historically significant figure, an African American who played in the U.S. Open in 1896, a trailblazer long before golf ever recognized that a trail needed to be blazed.

The PGA had a Caucasian-only rule until 1961, fourteen years after Jackie Robinson brought down the color barrier in baseball. The first African American to play in the Masters was Lee Elder, in 1975. In many precincts today, golf remains an exclusionary game.

Yet, more than a century ago, Shippen strode to the first tee at Shinnecock Hills Golf Club in Southampton, New York, to compete for the national championship, though he did not venture there unencumbered with controversy. There was even a debate over his heritage; he was thought to have been half black and half Indian, a part of the Shinnecock tribe from the land on which the course was built. His daughter, however, maintained later that he was 100 percent African American.

At any rate, he was a man of color, which in this or any other game of the era made him an outcast. He was joined by Oscar Bunn, who indisputably was a native American, a Shinnecock Indian. Each of them had entered the 1896 Open, to the chagrin of others in the field.

On the eve of the Open, several of the professionals entered met to decide what to do in the event Shippen and Bunn were permitted to play. Eventually, they decided to draft and sign a petition stating their intention to boycott the tournament, were Shippen and Bunn part of the field. The petition was delivered to Theodore Havermeyer, the president of the USGA, who, to his credit, declined even to take it under advisement. Shippen and Bunn were going to play, Havermeyer decreed, even if a boycott required that they play alone, a field of two. The boycott failed to materialize, and thirty-five players teed off in the first round at Shinnecock Hills, including Shippen and Bunn.

Shippen had assisted in the construction of Shinnecock Hills, was a caddie at the club, and was familiar with every step of the course, though the steps did not add to any significant number. At 4,423 yards, as it played in 1896, Shinnecock Hills was the shortest course in the history of the Open.

His knowledge of the course gave him an advantage on which he capitalized early. He shot a 78 in the morning round of the one-day, thirty-six-hole affair, and trailed the leader, Joe Lloyd, by only two. Through twelve holes in the afternoon eighteen, Shippen had played himself into a position to win. Then on the thirteenth hole, his bid unraveled.

"It was just a little easy par-4," Shippen said. "All I had to do was play it to the right, but I played it too far right and ended up on the sand road. I kept hitting it on the sand until I ended up with an 11."

That was a seven-over par 11, a number that dealt a fatal blow to his chances. The winner, James Foulis, ultimately defeated Shippen by those same seven deadly sins—extraneous strokes each of them.

This was Shippen's playing legacy and why he is remembered here. His was the single worst final-round crash by a U.S. Open contender in history, though not the most sensational, not once T. C. Chen gave history a lamentable reason by which to remember him.

The year was 1985 and the Open was returning to Oakland Hills Country Club, the Monster that Hogan had tamed in the final round of the Open in 1951. Oakland Hills would never again play as severe as it had then. Ten years later, in 1961, Gene Littler won the Open there with a seventy-two hole score of one-over-par 281, 6 strokes better than Ben Hogan's winning score there in 1951. The scoring average was more than 2 strokes lower in '61 than it had been in '51, as well.

Yet, Oakland Hills will never fall into the category of pitch-and-putt, either. In 1985, it remained a troublesome track that needed no difficulty-implant, yet the USGA, typically unable to restrain itself, performed one, anyway. On the eve of the tournament, Fuzzy Zoeller stood on one of Oakland Hills's greens and demonstrated how difficult they were going to be. He placed a ball about eight feet from the hole, then turned and tapped the ball in the opposite direction, uphill. The ball rolled for about two feet, before gravity applied the brakes, but only for a split second. The ball then reversed its course and began rolling back toward the hole, eventually missing it and rolling another three feet past it before coming to a stop.

"How do you like that, fellows?" Zoeller said to a group of bystanders. "I call that an awesome undulation. These greens are the most severe I've ever seen."

The greens were better suited for a billiards player than a golfer, Tom Watson said. "If you want any chance at all of getting close enough to the hole to make a putt," he said, "you've got to bank your iron shots off the humps in the green."

This is the kind of precision that no one is capable of ordering up on command and why Watson called Oakland Hills "the toughest course in the U.S. Open rotation. It is the toughest course we will play all year. There's no question about it. I don't expect anyone to be under par this week."

Jack Nicklaus arrived at Oakland Hills a week early in an attempt to befriend the legendary beast, but it was in no mood to entertain allies. "How can you get any feel for the greens when you're putting off the sides of hills?" Nicklaus asked rhetorically. "I had some six-foot putts with a three-foot break."

Oakland Hills was adequately prepared to defend its honor, when it was ignominiously sucker-punched by a visitor from the Far East. His name was Tze-Chung Chen, but for the sake of clarity when he played here, he was known by his initials. T. C. Chen hailed from Taipei, Taiwan, and had already won two national championships that year—the Korean Open and the Japan Open—which together don't add to the prestige and importance of the U.S. Open.

In the first round at Oakland Hills, on the 527-yard, par-5 second hole, Chen hit a strong drive, then faced 256 yards to the hole on his second shot, 235 yards to the front of the green, and an additional 21 to the pin. He pulled a three-wood and took a mighty swing, all 140 of his pounds behind it, and the ball headed in the precise direction of the flag. It alighted in front of the green, then rolled toward the hole, finally disappearing into the cup for the rarest of feats—a double-eagle, the only double-eagle in the history of the Open, in fact.

"When I heard the crowd," he said, "I knew that the ball would be pretty close, but I never thought it would be in the hole. I didn't know it until two guys told me as I walked onto the green."

The crowd to which he was referring was in fact nonexistent. It was more like a gathering, the people numbering ten or so, which accounts for their failure to generate enough noise to reflect the enormity of the feat. The name of the man who informed him of his double eagle? Ralph Eagle, coincidentally.

When the score was posted, the reaction was disbelief. "Maybe the scorekeepers got mixed up," one player said. "It's got to be a mistake."

The double-eagle (also known in golf as an albatross) provided the impetus in his round of 65, equaling the competitive course-record on a layout that Ben Hogan claimed to have brought to its knees, with a final-round 67 in 1951. It gave Chen a one-stroke lead over Fred Couples, the only other player to master the Monster in the first round. Andy North, who won the U.S. Open in 1978 at Cherry Hills, opened with an even-par 70.

"I am so surprised to be leading," Chen said through an interpreter. "It was such an honor just to be here. I was so happy I qualified, and now I am the leader. Tomorrow, I think I will come out and try to get the ball in the fairway, and then get the ball on the green."

That always has been the formula for playing well in a U.S. Open, where the penalty for missing a fairway or a green is the most severe in golf. The USGA, of course, shrinks the size of these targets by narrowing the fairways and making the greens so hard that a deft touch is required to keep a ball from scooting off into the fringe. This is the USGA's defense mechanism, the way it deflects otherwise quality-shots and causes scores to soar. At the very least, players are certain to miss fairways and greens at a debilitating rate.

The ruthlessness with which the USGA administers its championships manifested itself in another way in the first round at Oakland Hills. Denis Watson's ten-foot par putt on the eighth hole hung precariously on the edge of the cup, teasing gravity and seemingly unable to decide whether to stay or go. Ten seconds passed, then twenty, and thirty. Finally, thirty-five seconds after arriving on the rim and teetering on the precipice, the ball tumbled into the hole for what Watson assumed was a belated par.

Montford T. Johnson, the USGA's rules official with Watson's group, immediately informed Watson that the 4 he thought he had made was actually a double-bogey 6, the result of a two-stroke penalty for violating rule 16-1h, which allows only a ten-second wait for the ball to fall.

"The rule is a little cranky," Watson said. "The putt was ten feet, downhill, and the green was spiked up. I thought it was in, but it stopped, hanging over the cup. I walked up to see how close it was and said, 'I think it's still moving,' and backed off. It didn't fall, and I stepped up to knock it in when it fell in the hole. An official came up and told me I'd taken too long, that I'd stood there thirty-five seconds when the rule is ten seconds, whether the ball is still moving or not. That's the rule, so I was wrong, but I think the way it was handled was disappointing. It is the rule, but I think the people setting the rules get a little carried away sometimes."

Inflexibility is inbred in USGA officials—bloodthirsty creatures void of compassion. A proper pedigree cannot even buy immunity from the USGA's wrath, as the first thirty-six holes of the '85 Open demonstrated. The *Los Angeles Times* called it "the greatest carnage of name players in U.S. Open history." Jack Nicklaus was the headliner of a gilded cast that missed the cut. Tom Watson, the reigning PGA player of the year, also failed to advance, as did Masters champion Bernhard Langer, Lee Trevino, Ben Crenshaw, and Craig Stadler.

The leaderboard required introductions, considering the dearth of recognizable names there. Chen retained his lead and Jay Haas and Andy North were a stroke back. Rick Fehr and Dave Barr were also near the lead. From that group, only North had won a major championship, the U.S. Open, in 1978.

This again raised the argument as to whether the U.S. Open was in fact identifying the best players or was it introducing a degree of parity into the event by reducing the importance of various aspects of the game (i.e., long driving and chipping).

The most vociferous critics always occupy the media tent, writers seeking better play for their stories. "Bigger the name, better the headline," the writer Dan Jenkins once said. T. C. Chen might have been a compelling story in Asia, but in the United States, he was not even guaranteed a headline for leading the Open. One newspaper's headline on its U.S. Open story simply referred to it as the NO-NAME OPEN.

Another dilemma for the media was Chen's lack of mastery of the English language. For instance, he was asked what it would mean to him if he were to win. A puzzled look crossed his face. "Why would it be mean if I won?" he responded. It was an innocent reply with more truth than he could have known, given a press-corps rooting, not against him, but for an easier story to write than one on an unknown Taiwanese speaking rudimentary English at best.

Unknown leaders of any nationality have a way of depleting the drama from a tournament. Chen remained atop the leaderboard through fifty-four holes of an Open that was rapidly leaking interest and threatening to reach empty before Sunday's telecast began. The first four names on the board were Chen, North, Barr, and Fehr, all of them collectively responsible for invoking yawns for no other reason than that their names weren't Nicklaus, (Tom) Watson, Trevino, and Ballesteros. "To add a little drama to today's final round," the *Los Angeles Times* wrote, "Chen made two bogeys on the back nine to drop closer to North. With Jack Nicklaus, Tom Watson, Craig Stadler, Bernhard Langer, Lee Trevino and Ben Crenshaw already on the sidelines, this tournament needs all the drama it can find."

Stay tuned, as the man in the broadcast booth says.

The U.S. Open in 1985 seemingly was incapable of producing a memorable winner and opted instead for a memorable loser. This is the risk inherent in setting up a course so difficult that it invites embarrassment and failure—the elements that have led many to conclude that the Open is not a tournament you win so much as one that others lose.

When play began on Sunday, Chen had a two-stroke lead over North, with whom he was paired. Four holes into the final round, Chen increased the lead to 4 and seemed on the brink of draining the Open of whatever drama remained. Then fate intervened on behalf of the audience, rescuing the USGA from an indictment for committing apathy.

At the 457-yard, par-4 fifth hole, Chen had a long-iron second shot to the green and pulled a four-iron from his bag. He put a cock-eyed swing on it and pushed the ball well to the right. It missed the green by thirty yards and sunk into deep, thick U.S. Open-signature rough. His next effort, a flail designed simply to get the ball somewhere on the green, came up short, leaving his ball in the ratty green-side rough.

For his fourth shot, he took his sand wedge and attempted to pop the ball in the air to land it softly on the edge of the green, so that it would not scoot too far past the hole. He achieved the pop part, but his club got tangled in the grass and stuck for a split second before it broke free, accelerating his follow-through and causing his clubhead to hit the ball a second time while it was airborne. In effect, Chen had hit it twice with a single swing, a turn of fortune over which he understandably was aghast. Chen looked ashen as he pondered the error and his dramatically shrinking lead.

The swing counted for 1 stroke, and for striking the ball a second time in the course of a stroke, a violation of Rule 14-4, he was penalized a stroke. Moreover, the inadvertent contact deflected the ball away from the green. Now lying five and entirely unnerved, his thought processes short-circuiting, Chen attempted an heroic recovery chip, but the ball went seven feet past the hole. He missed the putt coming back and tapped in for—what? A rule book and a calculator might have helped at this point.

"I think I take eight there," Chen said to USGA president James Hand, who was the referee in the group.

"You are right," Hand replied.

It was indeed a quadruple-bogey 8—the damnable snowman from golf's lexicon—that erased his entire four-stroke lead in a matter of moments. Chen and North were then tied for the lead, while Canadian Dave Barr was a stroke back.

"T. C. opened the door for a lot of us right there," North said later.

"It was a freaky thing, but it's happened to a lot of us. I know he had a sickening feeling at the time."

Chen's faux pas injected the Open with the compelling angle it heretofore had lacked—the crash-and-burn plot. The double hit represented the crash. The ensuing three bogeys Chen made represented the burn.

"When I arrived today, I didn't feel what you call the Open pressure," Chen said afterward. "I was confident until the fifth hole. After that, all my confidence was gone."

Still, Chen remained in contention. North fumbled the gift he was presented, by bogeying three of four holes, elevating Barr to the lead. Barr's grasp was tenuous, as well; he bogeyed three of the final six holes. When Chen birdied the twelfth hole, he momentarily was tied for the lead, joining North and Barr, and positioning himself for a last-minute stay of execution.

But Chen bogeyed the thirteenth hole and three-putted from sixty-five feet to bogey the seventeenth hole, returning him to his place in the calamity division of Open lore. North, meanwhile, played the final seven holes in even par to conclude a round of 74, earning him a one-stroke victory over Chen, Barr, and Denis Watson and his second U.S. Open title.

North hit only 4 fairways in the final round and he made only 9 birdies over seventy-two holes, the least by any Open winner since World War II. His score of four-over par equaled the highest final-round score (in relation to par) by an Open winner since World War II. Sometimes, the course brings the winner to his knees.

Chen finished with an ignominious 77 that represented the injury augmented by the insult the media inevitably attached to his unraveling. His initials coincided beautifully with the misfortune that derailed T. C. Chen, and the media pounced. The T. C. no longer stood for Tze-Chung, but for Two-Chip. To this day, any mention of him will invariably entice someone to remember him as Two-Chip Chen.

"I finished second," Chen said, "and that is not too bad for my first time in the U.S. Open, and I made a lot of friends here. But I just played bad, pitiful golf today. After the fifth hole, the double hit was on my mind most of the way around."

Jim Murray wrote that the collective performance to which Chen contributed so dreadfully set golf back a hundred years. "It was the worst golf I ever saw in my life by guys who were sober," he wrote.

The footnote to this Open was that Denis Watson actually took the fewest number of strokes, 278. One could have guessed that, given the insidious nature of the game, that two-stroke delay-of-game penalty in the first round eventually would cost him the tournament. Watson's official score became 280 and he lost by a single stroke. "Golf," he said needlessly, "is a very tormenting game."

Tell it to Chen. Or to Shippen. The latter at least had the fortune of imploding in virtual obscurity, long before television had entered our living rooms, long before the U.S. Open was the showcase it has become. Chen's implosion occurred on international television—a sensational, if pitiable, episode that will be the standard by which all future final-round collapses will be measured.

A padded cell might have awaited him, but Chen proved more resilient than he was lucky. The mental damage was not permanent. Two years later, Chen defeated Ben Crenshaw in a play-off to win the Los Angeles Open.

Time is said to heal wounds. The caveat is that healing will occur only if you quit picking the scabs. For Chen, it will always remain an open wound, or an Open wound, as it were. A dozen years after the fact, the USGA produced a video and CD-ROM on the rules of golf.

To illustrate Rule 14-4, the USGA, ostensibly celebrating the pain and suffering it had caused, revisited for perpetuity Two-Chip Chen's most regrettable day in golf.

11

A DAY FOR A KITE

PEBBLE BEACH GOLF LINKS, 1992

The SOS (Save Our Shrine?) that went out on behalf of the Pebble Beach Golf Links in the run-up to the 1992 U.S. Open may not have been delivered in Morse code, though it would have been appropriate.

Pebble Beach was founded by Samuel F. B. Morse, grandnephew and namesake of the man who invented the telegraph and gave us the Morse code. Morse (the grandnephew) was an environmentalist, though not an infallible one. He was unable to resist the promise of profit, and permitted a sand-mining operation access to nearby Spanish Bay, despoiling the dunes there. Yet Morse rescued the cliffs and other seaside land at Pebble Beach from real estate developers or worse. "Without a Sam Morse," Bing Crosby once said, "there would be no Pebble Beach. It would all be Coney Island."

When Morse died in 1969, the course became something less than the treasured keepsake it ought to have been. It was treated as though it were just another piece of property to be bought and sold for a profit, rather than the crown jewel of American golf that it was, a place that had come to be known as the Sistine Chapel of golf.

Wedron Silica Company, which owned the sand mines that razed Spanish Bay, took over the Pebble Beach Corporation from Morse, then sold it to Twentieth Century Fox, a movie studio that had money to invest, but no apparent passion for what it invested it in. On deck was Marvin Davis, who in 1982 bought Twentieth Century Fox and all its assets—including the Pebble Beach Corporation—and began selling them off piecemeal.

In the late '80s, Davis attempted to sell the Pebble Beach Corporation for $1 billion, or nearly double what it was thought to have been worth at the time. Unable to find a buyer at that price, "Davis began a new policy at Pebble Beach, benign neglect," *Sports Illustrated* wrote. Former USGA president Sandy Tatum said it was apparent that in an attempt to increase cash flow, the cost of caretaking was substantially reduced and the course was "manifestly deteriorating."

Davis denied that his company was neglecting the course, blaming instead a drought for hampering efforts to improve conditions there.

It was indisputable that Pebble Beach had become tarnished. It had come to resemble a ramshackled public course usually found at the muny level, rather than a national treasure that ought to have received daily doses of spit and polish to enable it to retain its splendor.

"I'd call it neglected," said Grant Spaeth, later a USGA president and a Bay Area native who had known Pebble Beach intimately since childhood. "The greens had become shabby and the bunkers looked like they needed to be tended. It simply was not up to that ultimate standard."

The course had been infested by the sturdy, but weedlike and unwelcome kikuyu grass. Moreover, the bunkers had not been tended to and the greens had shrunk over time, as greens tend to do when mowing patterns are erratic and the fringe is permitted to encroach.

Those in the golf community were aghast at the state of disrepair into which Pebble Beach had fallen. Frank Hannigan, once the executive director of the USGA, was involved in the two previous Opens at Pebble Beach and likened efforts to coerce the ownership into improving its condition to pulling teeth. Too many rounds generating too much profit that would have eroded from too much costly manicuring kept the course in a perpetual state of disrepair.

In the late '80s, with the Open scheduled to return in 1992, Spaeth issued a warning to the company president Tom Oliver.

"Tom," Spaeth said, "in all due respect, looking at the course, I'm very worried. You have to get it in shape. This is serious stuff."

An influx of cash was required to resurrect its lost glory, and in September of 1990, Davis found a man covetous enough of the property to overpay for it. Davis sold it to a Japanese businessman, Minoru Isutani, for $841 million, a staggering sum thought to have been about $300 million more than it was worth at the time. Thus began a brief, but sordid chapter in the history of the most revered course on American soil.

Among Isutani's first orders of business was to ask Jack Nicklaus to redesign the Pebble Beach Golf Links. From the standpoint of Nicklaus, or anyone else who revered the course and its history, this was akin to asking that the Liberty Bell be discarded as a result of its crack and that it be replaced with a new bell.

"Whoa," Nicklaus said. "Nobody redesigns Pebble Beach. It's an American shrine."

The idea fortunately was abandoned by Isutani, who had other concerns. He had overpaid for the corporation at a time when the Japanese stock market was in free fall, interest rates were rising, and a global recession was gathering momentum. His investment immediately was recognized as a horrific one, though he developed a plan to rescue it:

He was going to sell private memberships in Pebble Beach, enabling him to recoup a significant portion of his investment.

The backlash to the plan was swift and violent. Its flaw—notwithstanding a public-relations nightmare—was that memberships might have significantly decreased public access to the course, an idea that was rejected by the California Coastal Commission. Unable to sell memberships, which would have enabled him to begin making payments on his enormous debt, Isutani was in a bind. By December of 1991, little more than a year after Isutani had purchased it, the Pebble Beach Corporation was declared delinquent in paying $3 million in property taxes.

Suddenly, six months before the U.S. Open was to be played there, Pebble Beach was haunted by the specter of bankruptcy—an alarming possibility and a potential embarrassment, given the scrutiny the national championship receives. The USGA's concerns were manifold. It even drew up a list of alternate sites in the event that Pebble Beach would be unable to fulfill its obligations.

In January of 1992, two Japanese companies—Sumitomo Credit Service Co., Ltd., and the Taiheiyo Club, Inc.—stepped in to rescue all involved. They bought the Pebble Beach Corporation for $574 million, renamed it the Lone Cypress Company, and essentially kept the Open from an ignominious last-minute relocation.

As for the condition of the course, Isutani had had the sense to retain Nicklaus to restore, rather than redesign, the Pebble Beach Golf Links. "We wanted to restore Pebble Beach to top condition while keeping its rustic and unkempt look," Nicklaus said. "We looked at a lot of old pictures and tried to recreate what was there from earlier days."

The pesky kikuyu grass was of particular concern. Overseeding with perennial rye was not an option; kikuyu was too strong and would win that battle. The only way to eradicate kikuyu is to kill it, and with the Open less than two years off, attempting to do so was a risky venture. They weighed the odds and placed their bet. "We took a big gulp," said RJ Harper, then the director of golf at Pebble Beach.

The kikuyu was sprayed with methyl bromide, which reduced Pebble Beach's fairways to dirt in a matter of days. It was then overseeded with perennial rye grass, which immediately took root, to the collective relief of those who had made the decision to eradicate the kikuyu.

Only later, when they could look back on the ordeal and laugh about it, Paul Spengler Jr., vice president of the golf division, was able to muse on what his legacy might have been had the experiment failed: "I'd go down in history as the man who killed Pebble Beach," he said.

When the players arrived for the '92 Open, they found a course that had been miraculously salvaged from the junk heap. "Gone are the sporadic patches of bluegrass, Poa annua and kikuyu that served as fairways," Ron Whitten wrote in *Golf World* magazine. "Gone, too, are the old tufts of grass atop sand that passed for rough, the old worn path that wandered between holes and the sandy scars of foot traffic around tee boxes. Instead, her holes are rolling carpets of gleaming ryegrass, her fairways meticulously striped, her rough distressingly uniform, her every hole framed by sturdy concrete paths complete with curbs. . . . There's no denying that Pebble Beach is in great shape, maybe the best shape of her seventy-plus years of existence."

The USGA, meanwhile, performed its own unique reconstructive surgery; it had grown the rough to penal heights, narrowed the fairways, and ensured that the greens were, as *Golf World*'s Bob Verdi wrote, "harder than *The New York Times* crossword puzzle."

"The winning spread should be between three strokes over par and three under par," the USGA's Sandy Tatum said. "Keeping par as a legitimate score is important. The idea is the Open is tough and it takes a tough guy to survive. We need to maintain that masochistic quality."

This is precisely what the players had come to expect. Davis Love III had not yet seen the setup, but he knew what was in store: "Deep rough and hard greens. It'll be just like the courses we see that are in good shape all year, until the USGA gets hold of it and makes it ridiculous."

The initial assessments of Pebble coincided with Love's prediction. "It's just my opinion," said Raymond Floyd, a former Open champion, "but they [USGA officials] take a marvelous links golf course like Pebble Beach, one everybody loves, and narrow the fairways and grow tall grass around the fairways and greens. Suddenly a links course I love is taken out of character. I don't appreciate it. Why not let the course get bare, dry, and hard and let the ball run where it should?"

This is how Pebble Beach once played. "It used to be a faster golf course," Spaeth said. "On holes like number eight, you used to bounce it on the green. Now you don't. It was a bit more Scottish then."

Spaeth was even of the opinion that rough was not necessary to the right of the fairway on the oceanfront holes. "I always felt that rough should not intervene between fairway and the ocean on four, six, eight, nine, ten, and I was overruled," he said. His idea was that without rough to impede the progress of a shot hit wayward right, the ball would bound off onto the beach, a greater penalty than simply finding yourself mired in the rough.

Roger Maltbie is a native of the Bay Area north of Pebble Beach and an aficionado of the course, which he regards as sacrosanct, a work of art, among the finest and most recognizable in the world until the USGA takes up a brush.

"If the USGA people took over the Louvre," he said, "they'd paint a mustache on the Mona Lisa."

The players' criticism seemed ill-advised, once the tournament began under overcast skies that typically create a windless condition. Twenty-nine players broke par and another sixteen equaled it in the first round. PEBBLE UNUSUALLY GENEROUS, said one newspaper headline.

Dr. Gil Morgan set the pace, shooting a six-under par 66, one of six rounds in the 60s. The scoring average was 74.5, nearly 3 strokes better than it had been in the first round of the '82 Open at Pebble and 3.5 strokes better than it had been for the '72 Open there.

The first round was further testimony on behalf of those suspecting the USGA had softened its resolve to put forth an annual test bordering on impossible. The average winning score in the 1980s had been 279.1, the lowest for a decade in Open history. Not once in the '80s was an Open won with a score of even-par or higher. The first two Opens in the '90s were won with scores of eight-under par (Hale Irwin at Medinah Country Club near Chicago) and six-under (Payne Stewart at Hazeltine). A record 124 sub-par rounds had been played at Medinah, 57 more than the second easiest Open.

"We are not going soft," USGA president Stuart Bloch said defiantly. "We had rain at Medinah right before the start and at Hazeltine last year, so the greens got softer and that made it easier to score. It was the weather, not the USGA, that caused it."

Morgan kept the USGA on the defensive by shooting a second round of 69, then birdied the third hole of the third round to become the first man in Open history to reach ten-under par. He birdied two of the next four holes as well, to reach twelve-under par, staking himself to a seven-stroke lead in the process.

Pebble Beach finally began counterpunching at that point. Morgan played the next eight holes in nine-over par, erasing his lead entirely. Only birdies on two of the last three holes enabled him to retain a slim lead.

"Will everybody bow their heads," Morgan said as he entered the media tent for a postround interview, jokingly offering a prayer for the deceased, which he nearly had become, figuratively.

"It was disastrous, wasn't it?" Morgan said. "I guess everybody else liked it. I kind of fell out of the sky. It felt like my parachute had a hole in it. After 7, I turned to my caddie and said, 'Well, here's where the golf course begins.' I probably shouldn't have said that. I thought 15 [under] would be a good number to get to, but then it just seemed to drift away."

Morgan would in fact expire the following day, when an early fog and gentle morning breeze soon gave way to sunny skies accompanied by gale-force winds upwards of thirty-five miles per hour that enabled Pebble Beach to defend its honor. The USGA provided an assist by depriving the greens of water, making them as hard as its heart. Morgan shot an 81, entirely erasing his strong work early in the week. He tied for thirteenth.

Even putting was difficult, beyond what it already was, without wind. "Putting was the hard thing," Colin Montgomerie said. "It's much more difficult than anyone can explain when your trousers are flapping and the ball's almost moving on its spot."

Richard Zokol was among the twenty players who failed to break 80. "It was just a massacre," he said. "Pebble Beach got even. You were afraid the ball was going to roll from a still position. It was the worst I could ever have imagined. I had no idea."

Scott Simpson was only three off the lead entering the final round, and shot an 88 to fall to a tie for sixty-fourth.

Raymond Floyd, among the critics at the outset of the week, had not changed his tune by the end of it. Even par and in contention entering the final round, Floyd shot an 81 and tied for forty-fourth. "It was ridiculous," he said. "There's no skill involved because of the greens. You saw the scores. It's not golf. And I don't think anybody wants to see that."

Nick Faldo was two strokes off the lead entering final-round play, and shot a 77. "It was impossible chasing [the leaders]," he said. "The course was not set up to chase. It just was enough to hang on. I hope they review the way they set up the golf course. If they like it, then fine. We're in trouble. But I think it needs reviewing. If they want greens like this, I'm going to take up topless darts, I think. It would be easier to catch them in your teeth today."

Faldo's ill humor was the result of more than just the difficult conditions. At the ninth hole on Sunday, his ball became buried in a bunker, forcing him to his hands and knees as he burrowed through the sand in search of it. Then, on the fourteenth hole, his errant approach shot stuck in an oak tree right of the green, forcing him to climb the tree in a futile search.

"In sixteen years as a pro I've never buried a ball in a bunker or had one stick in a tree, and then I do both in the six holes," he said. "Bloody ridiculous."

Not everyone was bedeviled. Montgomerie, teeing off a full two and a half hours before the leaders, was among four players to break par, shooting a 70 and finishing the tournament at even-par 288. A short time before that, Kite and Morgan each double-bogeyed the fourth hole and were tied for the lead at three-under par, three strokes ahead of Montgomerie. But each still had the bulk of Pebble Beach's trouble ahead of them, as well as Sunday Open pressure and fierce winds with which to contend.

Jack Nicklaus, who had missed the cut and was working for ABC Sports as a commentator on the weekend, was among those who were certain that Montgomerie had won the tournament, that with the wind and hard, fast greens, those still on the course would be helplessly unable to prevail. When Montgomerie arrived in the television tower behind the eighteenth green for a postround interview, Nicklaus shook his hand and said to him, "Congratulations, Colin. How does it feel to win your first Open?"

Nicklaus's clairvoyance had become something of a running joke among some PGA Tour members, who had nicknamed him Carnac, after Johnny Carson's *Tonight Show* character with all the answers, even before the questions were asked. Experience had provided Nicklaus the answer this time. Even Montgomerie had concluded that he was likely to win. He had noted earlier that the leaders were already three-over par early in their rounds, "and it wasn't getting easier," he said many years later. "I managed to bogey seventeen, which was a good result, and then par the last. And I must admit, I holed a very good putt at the last, about a five-footer, left to right, and I felt that I holed that putt to win. I felt, over the putt, that it was to win the tournament."

Kite, at the time, was in trouble at the par-3 seventh hole. The seventh hole sits on a parcel of land that juts out into Carmel Bay, exposed entirely to the elements. It is among the shortest, most picturesque, most spectacular, and occasionally most difficult holes in golf. It plays at 107 yards, from an elevated tee, a mere pitch-and-putt until the wind arrives to defend it, as it did that day.

Paul Azinger's tee shot there, for instance, landed so far left of the green that it came to rest on the eighth tee box. A sand wedge was the club of choice in the first three rounds. In the final round, six- and seven-irons were used.

The seventh was not a universally revered hole. Among its detractors was Ian Woosnam, the wee Welshman, who nearly triggered an international incident with his criticisms of Pebble Beach that week. Among his complaints was that there were too many blind shots. "At your height," the six-foot-three-inch Nick Faldo said to the five-four Woosnam, "I'm sure that's true."

When Woosnam saw the seventh hole for the first time, he was underwhelmed. "It looks like a little practice hole," he said. The print media feasts on controversy, of course, and Woosnam sated their appetite. When he arrived at the seventh tee on Sunday, a fan yelled, "Practice hole!"

The wind was blowing hard off Carmel Bay, gusting to forty miles per hour. Woosnam pulled his shot left of the green, then turned quickly to the gallery and barked, "Did you enjoy that one?"

The sea lies beyond and to the right of the green. Bunkers guard the front and the left of the green. When the wind is howling, as it usually is, it becomes a bantamweight champion. Sam Snead was said to have putted his ball from the tee box there once, to keep the ball beneath the wind, holding its vagaries in check, and allowing the ball to roll downhill into the bunker, from where it was probably easier to make par.

The wind was still blowing about forty miles per hour when Kite arrived on the tee box there, and though the target obviously is a stationary one, attempting to hit the green through the teeth of that kind of wind is akin to aiming at a moving target. For the task, Kite chose a six-iron that he attempted to punch in order to keep it low and under the bulk of the breeze. The ball missed the green long and slightly left, behind a bunker, and settled into thick rough.

"He probably had a fifty-fifty chance of getting it up and down [for par]," said his playing partner, Mark Brooks. "I walked past his ball, and he had a tough lie."

A steady nerve, deft touch, and more than a modicum of luck were required to successfully execute the shot, and Kite had all of them. His chip barely carried the bunker, bounced twice, then began rolling toward the hole with too much speed to sneak in. Eventually, the ball banged the flagstick dead on and dropped for a remarkable birdie.

"It was almost a shock when the ball went in," Kite said. "My first thought was, 'Yeah, Watson did it [on the seventeenth hole of the '82 Open at Pebble].' But he had only one more hole to play and I still had the entire golf course left. It turned out to be a big shot, but there were so many big shots left to play."

Nicklaus's congratulations had been premature, his timing horrible. "Kite chipped in and Jack turned his back on me," Montgomerie said.

Kite's improbable heroics were the third installment of historic shot-making at par 3s in the Opens at Pebble Beach. In 1972, Nicklaus nearly holed a one-iron shot on the seventeenth hole of the final round, cinching his victory. In 1982, Watson holed his difficult chip from thick rough to the left of the green at seventeen in the final round to defeat Nicklaus.

Kite fought Pebble Beach to a standstill in the final round. He played the final eleven holes in one-over par to conclude a round of even-par 72 in the worst of conditions, giving him a two-stroke victory and the first major championship of his career. "Those were probably the most difficult conditions to try to play in," Payne Stewart said years later, "and that's why Kite's round there could be one of the all-time greatest rounds of golf ever played."

Nicklaus's declaration that Montgomerie had won the U.S. Open missed its target and brought to mind a similar error in judgment made fifty-five years earlier, in the 1937 U.S. Open. When Sam Snead concluded the tournament at Oakland Hills in five-under par, Tommy Armour was there to congratulate him. "Laddie," the Silver Scot said, "you've just won yourself the Open." Alas, Ralph Guldahl was still on the course and charged in with a final-round of 69 to finish 2 strokes ahead of Snead, who never did win a U.S. Open.

Was history repeating itself? Montgomerie still has not won an Open. Nor has he won a major championship of any sort, earning him the tag that Kite shed with his victory at Pebble Beach in '92, *The best player never to have won a major.*

Kite was as relieved as he was euphoric over winning a major championship for the first time in twenty years as a professional. "It bugged the living daylights out of me," Kite said of those who criticized the absence of a major on his otherwise impeccable résumé. "It was like all the other things I've done didn't matter. Everyone seemed to think that if I didn't have one of those four tournaments under my belt I'd be suicidal. That wasn't the case."

He won the way he usually did—doggedly, though not necessarily spectacularly. He concluded seventy-two holes in three-under par 285, the highest number of strokes by an Open winner since 1978. The scoring average in the final round was 77.1, the highest since the '72 Open at Pebble Beach (78.8).

Years later, when he was presented with the notion that the ocean breezes demonstrate that Pebble Beach was not designed to accommodate the kinds of conditions the USGA introduces to the course for the Open, Kite smiled.

"To each his own," he said.

12

LITTLE BIG MAN

SHINNECOCK HILLS GOLF CLUB, 1995

The conciliatory note is not on the USGA's musical scale, which is reflected in the stern countenance its representatives wear so comfortably, however off-key. When a photograph of a scowling USGA president F. Morgan Taylor III once appeared on the cover of *Golf World* magazine, for instance, a foe from the equipment industry said he resembled I Duce.

Taylor's pose may have fit the acrimonious tenor of a debate on whether high-tech equipment was a threat to the game, but nonetheless it was an unflattering portrait framed by the question the magazine posed: Who is this man and why does he want to take your golf clubs away?

The stern countenance suggested that the answer was this: Because I can.

This is the aura the group sometimes transmits, creating an easy target for golfers attempting to deflect blame for their own misguided shots. The USGA's authoritarian demeanor represents a bull's-eye for critics with full quivers, and in the grand tradition of the elitist, it wears the arrows it absorbs as honorably as a martyr.

"Having critics shoot at the USGA is delightful," a former USGA president said once when his group was attempting to evade another incoming round.

Surely, then, the USGA must have held an emergency meeting of its executive committee to discuss where it went wrong at Shinnecock Hills Golf Club in Southampton, New York, when it took the Open there in 1986 for the first time since 1896.

The players overwhelmingly embraced it.

Good riddance is the reaction players typically have toward an Open course at the end of a long Open week, yet Shinnecock Hills generally avoided derision. Lee Trevino even said that should they decide to play the Open there again the following week, he'd happily return. When David Graham concluded a practice round that week, he encountered Frank Hannigan, the USGA executive director and the driving force behind bringing the Open back to Shinnecock. "Frank," Graham said, "you've finally done it. It's perfect."

Yet the USGA at large had gone there with reservations; it considered Shinnecock Hills as a risk from many perspectives, among them whether it was a representative test of golf for the caliber of golfer the game was now producing and arming with high-tech equipment.

"We didn't really know," said Grant Spaeth, a former USGA president. "Hannigan was of the view that even if the weather was great it was still a superb test of golf. Yes, they would shoot low scores. But there would be wind. It really was a sufficiently solid venue to accept an Open. Everything fell into place in a magical way."

The first time Tom Lehman played in an Open was in 1986 at Shinnecock Hills. "It was forty degrees, the wind was blowing forty miles per hour, and the rain was sideways," he said. "I looked over, and making the turn were Hale Irwin, Johnny Miller, and Seve Balles-teros, and the best of them was seven-over par. I thought to myself, 'I'm going to shoot 90.' That was my indoctrination into the U.S. Open."

The course indeed was a worthy antagonist, but one that commanded respect as well, and it was soon a fait accompli that the Open would return to Shinnecock Hills in the near future. The USGA decided on 1995, the one-hundredth anniversary of the organization, fittingly celebrated at one of its five founding clubs.

Shinnecock Hills was an anomaly that, from the standpoint of those given the charge of playing it, was a course so good that even the USGA was incapable of ruining it.

"You will not, in my mind, find one player, no matter where in the world he is from, who doesn't like this golf course the way it is set up," Raymond Floyd said on the eve of the '95 Open there. Floyd had won the '86 Open at Shinnecock. "It is truly a world-class course."

It, too, was a comfortable fit, demographically. The USGA stumbles when its attempts to argue convincingly that it embraces the notion that its game is an egalitarian one. Generally, the country clubs to which the sixteen members of the executive committee pay their monthly dues require blood of a bluish hue and the wherewithal usu-ally attached to such a pedigree—preferably old money at that.

Blue blood and old money form the cornerstones of Shinnecock Hills, which was built near the tip of Long Island in the posh enclave of Southampton, one hundred miles form Manhattan. William K. Vanderbilt, a scion of the railroad and shipping baron, was the princi-pal behind the construction of Shinnecock Hills, built on land once occupied by the Shinnecock Indians. Among those who frolicked on the original eighteen-hole playground there were financiers J. P. Mor-gan and Andrew Mellon.

A highway project forced the club to close the original course, and in 1930 a new one was designed by William Flynn and Howard

Toomey. Though it was not built on links land, it had the feel of a Scottish links course, with rolling hills, tall native grasses, and sea breezes.

"[Shinnecock Hills] more closely resembles a links than any course not really built on seaside ground," Robert Trent Jones wrote, "although it is close enough to get the ocean winds off two surrounding bays and Long Island Sound. There is a sweep and a majesty to Shinnecock that, along with its natural quality, puts it high among the world's best courses."

Johnny Miller, in his column for *Golf World* magazine, called it "shot for shot . . . America's best," though *Golf Digest*, in its biennial ranking of America's greatest golfers rated it number six. "If I were to choose sites for the United States Open," Miller wrote, "it would be easy. My Open lineup: one, Pebble Beach; two, Shinnecock Hills; three, Pebble Beach; four, Shinnecock Hills; five, Medinah. Every fifth year I'd throw in Medinah or Oakmont or Olympic Club. That's how good Shinnecock and Pebble are."

Miller even suggested that Shinnecock is capable of standing on its own, that the USGA need not disfigure it in its annual attempt to inoculate the Open site against a player assault. "Shinnecock is ready for a U.S. Open every day of the year it's open," he wrote. "They don't have to do anything. When I've been there on outings, the rough was two feet deep. Just cut the greens and they're ready for any Open any old day. This course doesn't need to be USGA-ized."

This assessment, however universal, failed to sway the USGA. For the '95 Open, the fairways were typically narrow—twenty-five to thirty yards—and the primary rough was five inches tall. Beyond that was the native fescue grass, a debilitating knee-high in length. "I hunt rabbits in that stuff," Fuzzy Zoeller said. "That's the beagle's job to go in there." Jungle grass, another player called it.

Yet even the USGA's signature flourishes to this masterpiece failed to dampen players' enthusiasm for playing the course.

On the three days preceding the Open, rain softened the course, but the greens were still rolling at 10.5 on the Stimpmeter, nearly the 11 for which the USGA was aiming. The weather was clear and the wind was en route. The wind brings out the British quality in Shinnecock Hills, arms it against those attempting to carve it up with their sharp shooting. "The wind," David Eger, the USGA's senior director of rules and competitions, told *Golf World* magazine, "is more of a factor at Shinnecock Hills than it is at any other traditional U.S. Open course, even Pebble Beach."

"I love the wind," said Tim Moraghan, championship agronomist for the USGA. "This weather is blowing out of here and we're going to have some fun."

An aside to the '95 Open was that Tiger Woods was making his U.S. Open debut there. Woods was nineteen and still an amateur who had qualified by virtue of his victory in the U.S. Amateur the summer before. Early in the week, Woods attempted to end the persistent line of questioning regarding his ethnicity by issuing a statement to the media. It read:

> *The purpose of this statement is to explain my heritage for the benefit of members of the media, who may be seeing me play for the first time. It is the final and only comment I will make regarding the issue. My parents have taught me to always be proud of my ethnic background. Please rest assured that is, and will be, the case. The various media have portrayed me as African-American, sometimes Asian. In fact, I am both.*
>
> *Yes, I am the product of two great cultures. . . . On my father's side I am African-American, on my mother's side I am Thai. . . . I feel very fortunate, and equally proud, to be both African-American and Asian.*
>
> *The critical, and fundamental point is that ethnic background and/or composition should not make a difference. It does not make a difference to me. The bottom line is that I am an American and proud of it!*

That is who I am and what I am. Now, with your cooperation,
I hope I can just be a golfer and a human being.

What he already was was a golfer of extraordinary skill, though those with whom he would play could not yet be considered his peers. Woods, as the Amateur champion, was paired with the defending champion and the British Open champion, Ernie Els and Nick Price, a pair whose talent reminded him that his game was not yet refined. "Let me put it to you this way," he said. "If I mis-hit a shot, I'm beaning the gallery. If they mis-hit a shot, they're just catching the green twenty feet away from the pin. Or if I mis-hit a drive, I'm in the hay and they're out on the first cut of the rough."

It proved to an accurate pre-tournament analysis. He was unable to find the fairway with the requisite frequency. He opened with a four-over par 74 that in part was the result of a wayward tee shot on the fourteenth hole, leaving him with an unplayable lie that led to a double bogey.

In round two, he was knocked out by the high fescue grass in which his ball landed on another misguided tee shot, at the third hole. When he attempted to muscle the ball out of the grass with a wedge, he sprained his wrist. Three holes later, he withdrew.

Woods may have been the complete package, but there was a growing concern that perhaps the package ought to have the word *fragile* stamped on it. In a six-month span, Woods had had arthroscopic surgery on his knee, a back spasm at the Masters, a strained shoulder muscle, and food poisoning. "He's a teenager who hasn't matured physically," his father, Earl Woods, said.

In truth, Tiger Woods was a victim of the penal nature of an errant shot in the U.S. Open. Another victim, more so from his own fragile psyche, was Ian Baker-Finch, the former British Open champion mired in a slump of career-ending proportions. He shot 83 and 82 in a pairing with Jack Nicklaus, who as a result invited him to stay at his house for two weeks so the pair could work on rehabilitating his game.

Shinnecock Hills, meanwhile, was putting up a spirited, if not remarkable, defense. "It's just plain scary," John Daly said, though his own aggressiveness off the tee, in concert with narrow fairways and high rough, routinely instills fear.

Greg Norman, a perpetual Open contender by now renowned more for the major championships he lost than the two he won, again put himself in position either to alter his legacy or to enhance it. He opened with rounds of 68 and 67, his five-under par total of 135 putting him two shots ahead of Japan's Jumbo Ozaki.

The relative docile manner in which the course responded over the first two rounds was in reality a setup for a Saturday that took its measure of the field and stamped this U.S. Open with the imprint of the USGA, even if it had not contrived to bring out the worst in men. "Obviously, we can't order the weather, although a lot of players think we can," said Eger, the USGA man responsible for setting up Shinnecock for the Open.

Yet, either by USGA writ or from nature finally imposing its will, the sea breeze stiffened to a degree that transformed the game into a brutal survival test. Tom Lehman said it was at least a two-club wind, and even a three-club wind at times, the difference between hitting, say, a seven-iron and a four-iron. It pushed airborne shots way off course and dried out the fairways and greens so that they played as hard and fast as the USGA expected they would. "It was," Ben Crenshaw said, "crash-and-burn day."

Massacre is a word that has earned a prominent place in U.S. Open history, given its ability to succinctly sum up a particularly grim day or week (see the Massacre at Winged Foot). *Sports Illustrated* dusted the word off for a piece it published on the third round of the Open at Shinnecock, calling it the Saturday massacre.

The course that day played like "an absolute bitch," Norman said. "I guarantee you, you've got no idea how difficult Shinnecock played today. I've been searching my mind when the last time was I've had such trying and difficult conditions, and I really can't remember.

"I can't remember ever seeing such great players humbled as what I saw out there today. You've got a very, very difficult golf course out here. I guarantee you, unless you played the course today, the commentators, the media, the spectators have got no idea how difficult Shinnecock played."

Even the USGA blamed the weatherman for dialing up too much wind. "We got more wind than we expected," Eger said, a curious excuse given Shinnecock Hills's proximity to large bodies of water and the wind inherent in such locales.

Downwind shots tend to reduce a ball's backspin, depriving it of its braking capacity. As a result, wind-aided shots hit to the hard greens at Shinnecock tended to skip over them. Crosswinds reduced an already scant margin for error from the tee, and shots were blown into the rough. The wind also dried and hardened the greens. "You could land 747s on them," Jeff Sluman said, regarding their firmness. This, of course, increased their speed, depriving players of the option of stroking putts with enough force to keep them on line. "You wind up hitting the ball so lightly," Phil Mickelson said, "it can't hold its line in the wind."

Greg Norman shot a four-over par 74, ordinarily a number that would cast a pall over a day. Norman instead was jubilant. "Sometimes shooting a 74 is as good as shooting a 62," he said, "and today was one of those days."

What, he was asked, was the equivalent of the three-under par 67 that Tom Lehman had shot (a score, incidentally, that enabled him to tie Norman for the lead at one-under par 209)?

"He shot 59," Norman replied.

Fuzzy Zoeller shot a 76 that wasn't as bad as it looked. He actually birdied a hole. "I'm lucky I didn't break any bones out there," he said. "I was in the hay all day. This course will just wear you out."

Scott Simpson was five yards from the green at number nine, his ball buried in thick cabbage. His attempt to gouge it onto the green failed, the ball moving only two feet, at which point he calmly took his wedge and bent it over his knee, the punishment it deserved for causing him so much anguish.

The wind blew so hard that Tom Watson lost his focus in the debilitating rough. He bogeyed four holes on the front nine, double-bogeyed the eleventh, and bogeyed the thirteenth and fourteenth.

"What I'd really like is a great big hot dog," Watson said to his playing partner Ben Crenshaw at that point. Watson continued to discuss the beloved frankfurter, eventually concluding that the best in the world are those offered in the snack stand by the fifth hole at Westchester Country Club.

"He just got to talking about hot dogs the rest of the way in," Crenshaw said. "And we were playing like hot dogs."

Tom Kite shot an 82, his worst round as a professional. It featured a pair of triple-bogeys, including one at the eighteenth hole, when his ball moved as he addressed what he thought would be his final stroke of the day, from a foot away. The rules required him to mark the ball, return it to its original position, and to assess himself a one-stroke penalty. When he failed to return the ball, he was assessed a second penalty stroke.

"I wasn't thinking very well at the time," he said. "When you're shooting 80 and standing over a one-foot putt, you aren't thinking."

Unless, of course, you're thinking about a hot dog.

The players' love affair with Shinnecock threatened to become strained by the wind. Phil Mickelson, a single stroke back, was concerned that the USGA was going to eschew watering the greens prior to the final round. "I can't believe they're going to let them get harder," he said. "It's going to be a joke watching these guys trying to play on these greens."

When Sunday arrived, pressure replaced the wind as the source of the players' torture in the final round. Coleaders Greg Norman and Tom Lehman each were even par for the tournament through the front nine, then stumbled on the back nine. Bob Tway, also even through nine, shot a back-nine 40.

Corey Pavin, meanwhile, was among the few players to benefit from the conditions. A dry, fast course negated the advantage longer players might have had over him on a wet course that would in all likelihood have played too long for him. An accomplished player with the void of a major championship on his record, Pavin hung around the lead for three and a half rounds, then birdied the twelfth and fifteenth holes on Sunday to get back to even par, maneuvering into a position to win.

When he reached the eighteenth hole, his lead was one over Norman, who was playing behind him. Pavin hit his drive into the fairway, leaving him 228 yards uphill to the pin, with a stiff wind blowing right to left. Pavin, the smallest man in the tournament, delivered its biggest shot, a four-wood second that stopped five feet from the hole and virtually clinched the Open championship for him. "I can't think of any shot that I might have hit better under pressure than that one," Pavin said.

A few hours later, Pavin and his entourage climbed onto the roof of the oldest clubhouse in the United States, designed by the preeminent architect of his day, Stanford White, and sat down and drank champagne to celebrate the victory by golf's little big man.

Everyone else had gone home, disappointed surely, but only at the way they had performed. Pavin's winning score was even-par 280, the first time the winner had not been under par since 1979. Shinnecock Hills was the other winner that week, by playing exceedingly difficultly, yet earning the players' respect.

"Most years at the Open you know the players will complain about something," Eger said before the players arrived. "Maybe this is the year they won't."

They didn't. "You run out of superlatives for this course," said Ben Crenshaw, golf's resident historian and a student and aficionado of architectural genius. "It really is one of our nation's finest courses, pure and simple."

The players' only legitimate complaint was a complimentary one: that the Open would not return to Shinnecock Hills for another decade or so.

13

WINDMILLS AND CLOWNS' MOUTHS

THE OLYMPIC CLUB, 1998

The USGA enjoys the opportunity to exert its authority, as it has been known to do by choosing not to cut a walkway from one green to the next tee, thus requiring that players slog through thick rough even after holing out. The USGA argues that it has done this as a pointed way of reminding the players that this is the U.S. Open, not the B.C. Open, as though they need a reminder beyond their struggle to break 80 each day.

The tyranny with which the USGA governs seemingly is designed to evoke humility, which brings us back to the Olympic Club, this time for the 1998 U.S. Open. The Olympic Club had already established beyond a doubt its ability to remove the sheen from the game's elite, reminding them that their immortality exists only in a figurative sense.

Surely, this has contributed to the USGA's love affair with the Daly City, California, course. The Olympic Club was dependable; each of the three previous Opens to which it had been home were defined far more by its losers than its winners.

The first involved Jack Fleck's ignominious derailing of Hogan's bid to win an unprecedented fifth U.S. Open title in 1955. The unknown Fleck defeated the great man, head to head, in an eighteen-hole play-off.

The Open returned to the Olympic Club in 1966, where Arnold Palmer took a seven-stroke lead to the back nine on Sunday, proverbially the place where a major championship is said to begin. Certain that he had won his second Open, Palmer began pondering Hogan's Open scoring record of 276 and decided that that would be a worthy memento to take away from the Open, along with the trophy. To equal the record, he needed only to shoot a two-over par 37 on the back nine.

Generally, the U.S. Open repels those strutting from overconfidence, as it did this time. For Palmer, it was the back nine on Sunday that the Open began to go wrong. The first couple of errant shots Palmer hit sucked the oxygen from him, and he began, in the parlance of the game, to choke. "Arnie just panicked," Billy Casper told *Golf Digest*. "I had never seen him panic before. He just kept pulling it left. He pulled it left at sixteen, left at seventeen, left at eighteen. Before that, he looked like he was cruising. He just panicked when I started catching up."

Palmer played the back nine in 39, while Casper played it in 32 to erase the entire deficit and force a Monday play-off that Casper won by 4 strokes.

"Arnie," Casper said as the pair walked from the green, his arm around Palmer's broad shoulders, "I'm sorry."

No apology was forthcoming from the USGA, which never knew an icon it could not take down, as it illustrated again when it took the Open to the Olympic Club for the third time, in 1987. This time, it was Tom Watson's turn in the Olympic shredder. A graduate of nearby

Stanford, a certifiable golf legend, he led by one through three rounds and was tied on the back nine on Sunday. Scott Simpson, however, birdied 3 consecutive holes on the back nine and beat Watson by a stroke, depriving him of his ninth major championship.

The Olympic Club is the graveyard of champions and, as such, surely has endeared itself in perpetuity to the USGA. It has small greens and infernal trees encroaching on the fairways and swatting down any shot that is marginally off line.

For the 1998 Open, the USGA applied its usual ghoulish touches: It heightened the rough, narrowed the fairways, and, to borrow the words that earned CBS's Gary McCord a permanent banishment from Augusta National, bikini-waxed the greens.

"It's almost like a race-car driver," Tom Meeks said. "We're living on the edge. We're trying to make it as hard as we can while being fair."

The difference is that the USGA officials are not behind the wheel on a dangerous track, instead presenting the players with the opportunity to crash and burn while they look on enthralled.

The rough at Olympic was not as penal as it had been when Hogan disappeared into it left of the eighteenth fairway in 1955, reemerging too late to win his fifth Open. It was frightening nonetheless. "I don't think you'll want to go into the rough too often," defending champion Ernie Els said. "You might break a couple of wrists or ankles out there." David Duval simply described it as brutal. "What else do you want, really? It's such that you can't progress the ball to the green."

The rough was unavoidable, however. The fairways were slender, certainly, but the myriad rolls and swales squeezed them to decidedly uncomfortable widths. "When you're really nervous," said Tom Lehman, "these fairways look like they're an inch wide because of all the slope in them."

Among those disoriented was the USGA. The organization had not been part of the PGA Tour's losing courtroom bid to disallow Casey Martin the use of a cart, but magnanimously it chose to "abide by the spirit of the court decision" and to permit Martin to use a cart in the Open. However, it declined to provide him the basic two-seat cart every club has, instead equipping him with a single-passenger cart, the kind you might find for the disabled at a supermarket.

"I knew it wasn't going to work," Martin said, though he gave it an effort. The severity of the sloping fairways made it treacherous going on such a small cart. As he drove up a hill toward the second tee box, "I just about flipped it," he said. "It was so small I kind of popped a wheelie."

When he felt the front wheels lift off, he hopped out and walked the next two holes. Finally, tournament officials provided him a traditional cart and agreed to let him use it during tournament play.

The slopes that nearly toppled the Martin Mobile, in conjunction with how firm and fast they were, made a journey around the Lake Course at Olympic similar to wearing leather-soled shoes and attempting to navigate your way across an ice rink, Nick Price said.

The USGA also chose to add sand to the bunkers to make them fluffy, increasing the difficulty of playing from them. Over time, the sand in bunkers tends to get compacted, making it an easy mark for tour players' bunker skills. "We are very much interested in having bunkers be more like hazards," USGA president F. Morgan Taylor III said.

The superintendent at the Olympic Club is John Fleming, whose father had been an associate of renowned architect Alister Mackenzie. "We've become so skilled at grooming and maintaining sand bunkers that the shot out of a bunker by these geniuses has been almost a guaranteed up and down," Fleming said. "A bunker by definition is a hazard, and I approve of what the USGA is trying to do. This year you'll find the sand in the bunkers softer."

When Mark Calcavecchia learned of Olympic's importation of sand, he rolled his eyes and provided an opinion to match the gesture. "So, when we fly it into the bunkers we'll be buried up to our ankles?" he asked rhetorically. "Yeah, why not? Ten-inch rough and new sand. Sounds like a USGA combo."

The more enterprising players in the field had had sand added to practice bunkers at their home courses to give them an opportunity to prepare to counter the USGA's perceived insanity.

The best preparation for playing any Open, however, is honing your attitude by expecting the worse and accepting the fact that this is probably what you will encounter. Beyond that, anything of a positive nature is a bonus. "I come to the U.S. Open expecting nothing to be fair," former Open champion Lee Janzen said. "So, it's a test of wills to find out who overcomes adversity the best and who has the most patience."

Once again, the USGA chose to transform the seventeenth hole from a par 5 into a par 4 for the Open, though the players refused to accept it as a reasonable interpretation of how the hole should play for them. "It's brutal," Justin Leonard said. "It's a par 5." Ernie Els said, "I don't think you'll find a much harder par 4 in the world."

Jack Nicklaus had the best summation: "The seventeenth is basically a way to get from the sixteenth green to the eighteenth tee."

Payne Stewart crushed a drive there in a practice round and still had a three-wood to the green. The obvious inference then is that, "it's a par 5." Janzen said it might be the toughest hole he's ever played in an Open.

The USGA alleviated the problem it had with the hole in 1987, when it also played as a par 4, at 428 yards. The problem with the hole then was that the landing area for tee shots was on a part of the fairway that sloped severely from left to right. The perfectly struck drive down the left side would simply succumb to gravity and bound down through the fairway and into the rough on the right. The only way to keep it from doing so was to drive in the left rough. In other words, the fairway was there strictly as decoration.

For the '98 Open, the hole was lengthened to 468 yards, all of it uphill, and the tee box was moved to a place that made the landing area relatively flat, but so far from the green that reaching it in 2 shots often was questionable. "I play that hole as a par 5," one player said. "It is ridiculous to sit there and psych yourself up and think, 'Hey, I'm going to make four here every day.' For me I don't feel like it's going to happen."

"If this hole is 468 yards," Nick Price said, "then I want to buy some real estate from the USGA."

Moreover, the green was designed for a short third shot on a par 5. It is diminutive and not particularly receptive to long-iron or fairway-wood second shots.

"Seventeen," Scotland's Colin Montgomerie said in summary, "is too long for four and too short for five." The USGA, of course, will always opt for the more difficult par. Germany's Bernhard Langer simply labeled it "the worst golf hole I've ever played."

The USGA argument is that par is irrelevant, that only a player's score on a particular hole matters. This is not necessarily true. Par *does* matter if it matters to the players. This, of course, is why the USGA operates in such a manner. It not only puts land mines out there, but it also engages in psychological warfare.

"The whole thing is a head game the USGA likes to play with us," Nick Price said. "If you let it bother you, it's another way in which you've let the course beat you."

When play began on Thursday, the course responded as expected. Frank Lickliter actually bent the shaft on his sand wedge attempting to muscle a ball out of the rough on the fourth hole.

After putting out on eighteen and concluding a long and disturbing round of 75, David Duval was escorted into the Olympic clubhouse and down a flight of stairs to an area where players signed their scorecards. "Are they taking us down here to execute us?" Duval asked, finding humor in a humorless environment.

Payne Stewart set the early pace, shooting a four-under par 66 that included an unlikely birdie three at the difficult seventeenth, for which he congratulated himself on making eagle.

Seventeen began the week as the most intimidating hole on the golf course, but by Friday afternoon it had been upstaged, at least on the notoriety front, by the eighteenth, a tiny, yet ferocious par 4, measuring only 347 yards and reachable with a long iron from the tee and a short wedge to the green. The green, however, slopes severely, back to front, and is small and closely guarded by gaping bunkers.

The size of the green there proved troublesome for the USGA. The organization requires consistency from Open greens, so if one is hard and fast, it prefers that they all play that way. But eighteen at Olympic is a small, narrow green that slopes adversely, substantially inhibiting the USGA's ability to find four suitable pin placements, one for each round. Typically, it would have two-back and two-forward placements, but the severity of the green's slope, as well as the hardness of the green, created a risk in putting the pin back even once.

But forward pins on all four days would wear out the green from the heavy foot traffic, creating a bumpy and unpredictable surface on which the Open might ultimately be decided. "We certainly didn't want to use that location on Sunday, because if a player has an eight-foot putt to win the U.S. Open, he ought to have a fair chance to make it," said Tom Meeks, the USGA's director of rules and competitions and the man ultimately responsible for pin placements. The USGA eventually decided it would put the pin back for one round only—the second—then hold its breath that it would suffice.

"Once one group played it," Meeks said, "I knew it wasn't going to work. It was a very hard hole location, and we were concerned about it, but we couldn't use the front all four days. The last thing we want is for a ball to go up toward the hole and then come back. It happened to a few players, unfortunately."

Kirk Triplett was among them. Frustrated when his ball started backtracking away from the hole, he put his putter out to stop it, incurring a two-stroke penalty. "I suspect he was trying to make a statement," said David Fay, USGA executive director who also was involved in the decision process on pin placements. "I think he felt he wasn't making the cut. He knew what he was doing. It was trunk-slamming time." Triplett only said, "That was just the last frustration of a frustrating day that wasn't really golf."

Several other players, with uphill putts that missed, also were startled to see their ball begin a retreat back toward them, only to stop mercifully before it rolled all the way down to the front of the green.

When Payne Stewart arrived there late in the afternoon, the pin placement was mocking the players. Stewart had hit a reasonably accurate pitching wedge second shot to ten feet right of the hole. His birdie putt narrowly missed the hole, but rather than leaving him a tap-in par, the ball never bothered to stop. Ever so slowly, it veered left and began a laborious trip downhill, the ball's logo disappearing and reappearing, over and over, seemingly in slow motion—a journey that by one estimate took twenty-two seconds—the ball finally stopping twenty-five feet from the hole. A short birdie putt had turned into a long par-putt.

Stewart was remarkably restrained, though perhaps only as a result of his befuddlement at what he was witnessing. He stood staring intently, arms folded, his jaws working frenetically on a piece of chewing gum, as he watched scornfully while gravity worked its black magic on his ball. That putt became the hallmark of the second round, the shot most often replayed on newscasts that night, the shot that became exhibit A in the argument that the USGA goes too far.

"That pin is cute, very cute," Stewart said as he came off the course. "I'll use other descriptions in the locker room. It was bordering on ridiculous. Curtis [Strange] hit a putt up there today and once it stopped it rolled back about six, eight inches. That is a little bit suspect in my opinion."

Bordering on the ridiculous was a generous assessment, surely. "Whenever you start seeing balls roll up to the hole and then roll back away from the hole, I think that is bordering on ridiculous. I think that that becomes almost—I don't know if the USGA would use the term 'an illegal pin.' I don't think I was the only one who spoke to the USGA walking official about that pin today, either."

If you make a putt there, Stewart was asked, do you get a free round, á la miniature golf courses with windmills and other assorted trickery?

"You know, I was watching the Putt-Putt championships this morning on ESPN and it resembled that a lot," he said.

He was asked whether there was any other way he might have played that putt (short of holing it) that might have prevented it from winding up so far below the hole.

"I guess I probably needed to play a big rainbow, maybe two feet of break and just let it die down there [by the hole]. I probably played eight inches of break. When I missed, I figured the ball would stop about two feet from the hole. The rest is history."

Stewart would have had a three-stroke lead had he made the birdie putt. Instead, he wound up with a one-stroke lead that he said "left a bitter taste in my mouth."

John Daly, never shy about expressing an opinion when asked for it, was given an opportunity to deliver his assessment of that pin placement at eighteen. He did not disappoint. "If they want to have a major, we can go to Disney World and play Putt-Putt," he said. "Thank God our tour doesn't do that. That was absolutely stupid. We work too hard out there. People [watching] on TV have got to think, 'these guys are idiots.'"

New Zealand's Frank Nobilo said it was the worst pin position he had ever seen in a major championship. When his thirty-five-foot uphill putt expended its energy, it began to retreat back down the hill toward him, eventually traveling twenty-five feet before stopping. "My ball was one roll from going all the way to the front of the green," Nobilo said.

Tom Lehman took 4 putts on the eighteenth green, then uncharacteristically berated a USGA official. "The people who set up this course are full of it," Lehman said to him. "Tell them that, OK? The eighteenth green was hard as a rock." When a reporter asked whether he would consent to an interview, Lehman replied, "Give me half an hour, or I might kill somebody."

"John Daly hit a putt that rolled up, almost went in and rolled back three feet [away] from the hole," Fred Couples said. "I personally think it's embarrassing. I mean, [USGA officials] should hit putts. They should put the pin there and hit a ball up there."

The USGA at least was forthright in acknowledging that, its history of malevolence notwithstanding, it had erred. "We made a decision and it didn't turn out the way we hoped," David Fay said. "We felt if we manipulated the mowing process and put more water on that hole than on the other seventeen we could manage it. We didn't expect that the turf, that the conditions would get away from us as much as they did. We felt that was the best location to have in the back. To have a location anywhere else would just magnify the problem. As it turned out, I think it's safe to say that if you were above the hole it was extremely difficult. The same way if you were beside the hole."

Meeks admitted to violating his philosophy on setting hole locations: If you have any doubts, don't use it. "I had doubt and I went ahead," he said. "I was forcing myself to make it work, and that's where I screwed up.

"I just hope no one thinks this hole was picked intentionally to see those balls do that. Most of the people sitting there yesterday probably liked seeing those players do that. I sat there and by this time it's starting to hit me, that really I've screwed this thing up. I sat there and was embarrassed that what was happening did happen because of what I'd done. I know better. I had my doubts. I thought it might work because we had made some different preparation. The bottom line was it didn't work.

"Unfortunately I'm probably going to be known when I retire as the guy who set the bad hole on Friday on the eighteenth of the 1998 Open."

It conceivably might have cost Stewart the U.S. Open, a tournament that does not readily forgive miscues, instead choosing to amplify them. Stewart's quality play early in the week began to give way to U.S. Open conditions and pressure. On each round, he hit fewer greens in regulation than he had the previous rounds. The number of putts he took went up.

Stewart was finally undone when his tee shot at the twelfth hole rolled onto a sand-filled divot in the middle of the fairway. He was stymied, even by a perfect shot. "In my opinion," he said, his protest going unheard, "that was ground under repair." For his second shot, he chopped the ball out and into a greenside bunker, then received a slow-play warning from Meeks at an inopportune time, just as he was on the verge of boiling over, anyway. Ultimately, Stewart missed an eight-foot par-putt to fall out of the lead for the first time since Thursday.

Tiger Woods was among those unable to uncover a solution to a bewildering problem. "When you put pins on the sides of hills and the rough is completely unforgiving, then you create a situation where anything can happen," Woods said, his own bid to win the Open falling well short.

Lee Janzen's U.S. Open attitude, meanwhile, paid dividends. Janzen was playing well, grinding his way into contention, but never losing sight of what might happen in a U.S. Open. Expecting the worst, he encountered it when he pushed his four-wood tee shot on the fifth hole toward the trees right of the fairway. When Janzen arrived at the tree, he discovered that his ball had stuck in its branches. Once he identified the ball, he began walking back to the tee to hit another, when a gust of wind miraculously dislodged his ball, saving him from a stroke-and-distance penalty for an unplayable lie.

"I went from lucky-to-make-a-double to walking away from that hole with a par," Janzen said.

After this fortuitous turn, "You could tell he was on a mission all of a sudden," his playing partner Steve Stricker said. "He started striding down the fairways with a purpose."

Janzen played the back nine in two-under par, and he parred the last five holes, a Herculean effort on Open Sunday, to beat Stewart by a single stroke, one that could be traced to that curious three-putt on the eighteenth green on Friday.

The 154 players in the field averaged 1.99 putts on the eighteenth green on Friday. Their average for the other seventeen greens was 1.66

putts. Stewart had been its most visible victim, incurring what was tantamount to a stroke penalty for an error not of his doing, yet he took his defeat in stride, declining to blame it on either his rotten luck on Friday or Janzen's good luck on Sunday.

"I got beat by a great round of golf," he said, regarding Janzen's closing 68 that resulted in a winning seventy-two hole score of even-par 280.

In fact, he and everyone else who came up short got beat by a great golf course injected with an overdose of the USGA's mean medicine. The seventeenth hole, for instance, yielded just 9 birdies in four rounds. The scoring average was 4.718, nearly equal to the scoring average on the first hole—a par 5. Players hit the green in regulation only 22 percent of the time at seventeen, a demonstration of mismarksmanship that one would more likely find on Saturday morning at nearby Harding Park, a bedraggled muny course.

"I didn't think I'd say this," Ernie Els said, "but this is the hardest golf course I've ever played. You couldn't do anything right this week, especially over the weekend."

Els closed with a 76, signed his card, then made his way to a corral area to address the media. "All right," he said addressing the gathering, "shoot . . . me."

Lehman closed with a 75 that included at least one baffling putt, resulting in this exchange.

"Is it uphill or downhill?" Lehman said to his caddie, Andy Martinez.

"I don't know," Martinez replied.

"Well, I guess we're in trouble," Lehman said.

It was an imperfect test from the players' standpoint. "The thing that I disagree with is that not all parts of the game were tested," said Phil Mickelson, a long hitter with a creative short game. "I don't think the driver was tested because you couldn't use it. I don't think the short game was tested."

Mickelson was among the players who took his driver out of his bag that week, essentially removing the temptation to use it on Olympic's perilously narrow and undulating fairways. Colin Montgomerie discarded his driver as well.

"The only way the USGA could prevent scores in the low 60s was to trick it up," wrote Derek Lawrenson in the British paper the *Sunday Telegraph*. "All you need to know about the course setup is that Colin Montgomerie, who is usually considered the straightest driver in the world, did not bother to take the driver out of the boot of his car over the first three days. Was that how this course was designed to be played?"

"This U.S. Open became a caricature—at least a prototype—of so many Opens played before it," John Hawkins wrote in *Golf World* magazine. "It stood out mainly in the sense that it included so much of what has come to define our national championship: tedium, controversy, luck, a winning score of even par, a leaderboard full of U.S. Open-type players . . ."

The Open, in all likelihood, will return to the Olympic Club some day, but not before the eighteenth green has been rebuilt to give the USGA more pin-placement options. "The eighteenth green is a real issue and before we would take it back [to the Olympic Club] it has to be resolved," said Dr. Trey Holland, a former USGA president, upon visiting the course nearly two years later. "They are willing to fix it. And if we decide to go back we feel comfortable saying that we will come back contingent on fixing this green."

Stewart's three-putt there on Friday ultimately cost him the championship, and the USGA clearly was embarrassed, a new experience for an organization that prefers that whatever pain it generates is not self-inflicted.

For once, the USGA was a victim of its own malice.

14

PAINHURST

NO. 2 COURSE AT PINEHURST

Superficially, it might be concluded that course architect Donald Ross never fully understood the game of golf, even as he was weaned on it at Dornoch in Northern Scotland and later in an apprenticeship served under Old Tom Morris at St. Andrews. Ross had the misguided notion that "golf should be a pleasure, not a penance." What, the USGA might have asked in a moment of candor, could he have been thinking, pleasure not penance?

The nineteenth hole was designed to soften the pain inflicted by the previous eighteen, the only evidence required to establish the fallacy that pleasure has any place in the game. Of course, golf is a penance. The USGA understands this intrinsically.

A more extensive examination of Ross's philosophy reveals that he believed whatever pleasure one might derive from the game was not to be a gift, but a reward. The alterations he made to his original design of the No. 2 Course at Pinehurst reflected this theory.

"As a result of extensive changes," he wrote, "I am firmly of the opinion that the leading professionals and golfers of every caliber, for many years to come, will find in the Number Two Course the fairest yet most exacting test of their game, and yet a test from which they will always derive the maximum amount of pleasure."

The U.S. Open had never before been played at Pinehurst for a variety of reasons, none of them relating to an inability of the course to present a stern, fair test. Ross built stern and fair into the No. 2 Course, which ranks among the finest work of his distinguished architectural career.

Ross once said, "Give me some slightly rolling terrain and sandy soil, and I'll give you the best courses." He found both in the Sandhills of North Carolina, where the sandy terrain enabled him to build a course unique to design in America.

Pinehurst's most prominent feature is its crowned greens, loosely described as resembling inverted cereal bowls. Balls that miss the green by a matter of inches will roll down into hollows and swales surrounding the green. The sandy terrain enabled him to design these kinds of greens that would have presented drainage problems on courses with less porous soil.

"The problems which he presented to those who play his courses were not of the obvious and spectacular sort," Pinehurst president Richard Tufts once said of his designer. "There was nothing vulgar about his work."

There was, instead, genius at work, his ability to find a way to challenge expert golfers while at the same time not substantially punishing average ones as a result. "These are the best set of greens in golf," *Golf Digest*'s architectural editor, Ron Whitten, wrote. "Average golfers who miss a lot of greens anyway aren't affected, but skilled players can be."

The No. 2 Course evolved into perhaps Ross's most famous work.

He was said to have been disappointed that Bobby Jones had selected Dr. Alister MacKenzie to design the Augusta National, a project he was said to have coveted. He ultimately decided that if Pinehurst No. 2 was destined to be his signature course, he was determined to continue refining it in an attempt to achieve perfection.

Ross even moved into a house adjacent to the third fairway, and he continued to make subtle changes to the course until he died in 1948, more than forty years after the course had been built.

One reason the Open had never before been played at Pinehurst was that the USGA considered it too remote. Moreover, the late Richard Tufts, president of Pinehurst and part of the family that had owned it from 1895 through 1970, was not particularly fond of professional golfers.

The PGA Championship, however, was played there in 1936, when Ross wrote an analysis that would have held up sixty-three years later. "I am sure as you watch the play," he wrote, "you will be interested to see how many times competitors whose second shots have wandered a bit will be disturbed by these innocent-appearing slopes."

Another professional tournament, the North and South Open, was played there until 1951, the year the Ryder Cup was played on No. 2. But when virtually the entire U.S. Ryder Cup team declined to remain behind to play in the North and South, Tufts was duly angered enough to cancel the event after that. "The happy, friendly atmosphere of the old North and South had vanished," he said, "and it seemed that the money-changers had taken possession of this particular temple of golf."

Tufts once was a USGA president who embraced the traditions of the organization, including those that were condescending of the professional golfer and celebrated the amateur. Accordingly, the U.S. Amateur was played there in 1962, and when gallery ropes were placed, they were placed well beyond the fairways, back in the trees. When Tufts was asked why, he replied, "This event is for the players, not the fans."

When Pinehurst was sold to the Diamondhead Corporation in 1970, the new ownership returned professional golf to No. 2, with the World Open. The new owner thought it could improve on a Donald Ross design and began replacing the sand and pine needles bordering the fairways with Bermuda rough. For the tournament, the rough was allowed to reach four inches in height, requiring anyone missing a fairway to simply gouge his ball back to the fairway.

The rough notwithstanding, Johnny Miller shot a 63 in the second round of the World Open there in 1974.

"Johnny," a reporter said to him, "you're not supposed to shoot 63 on this course. That's why they let the rough grow."

"I know," Miller replied, "but when you're shooting 63 you're not in the rough."

The owner also replaced the Bermuda grass on the greens with bent grass, the strains of which at the time were not sturdy enough to withstand the summer heat. This, in concert with the fact that Pinehurst lacked proximity to a metropolitan area, conspired against this work of art ever appearing in the U.S. Open gallery.

When Club Corporation of America took over Pinehurst in the early '80s, it restored it to its former prominence. Even the professionals were invited to return, with the Tour Championship in 1991 and 1992, and with the U.S. Senior Open in 1994. What the USGA learned from observing these events was that the greens were still not good enough to withstand a full-field assault, especially in the heat of the summer.

The USGA agreed to take the Open there for 1999 with the understanding that the greens would be overhauled. Eventually, they were restored to their original size and covered with a new strain of bent grass, Penn G-2, which could play fast and withstand summer heat and humidity, drought, and heavy play. Even in the event of heavy rain, they come equipped with a portable pump system to suck the moisture from them.

Over time, the Bermuda fringe had encroached on the bent-grass greens, eventually reducing them to the point where they fit on the plateau of the crown, diminishing the effect of the slopes. Before they were restored, shots that just missed the green hung up in the fringe, rather than gathering speed and rolling down into the hollows.

For the Open, the banks around the greens and on the swales and hollows were also resurfaced with hybrid Bermuda that was cut to fairway length and rolled to make them hard and fast and incapable of stopping a ball from descending into the collection area.

"There are days when, if you miss a green at Pinehurst, you spend the rest of the afternoon trying to get the ball back on," Jack Nicklaus told *Golf Digest*. "That's the way I think Pinehurst should be."

Thus, short-game skills returned to the equation when the Open went there in 1999. Typically, the USGA orders long, thick rough around the greens, effectively neutralizing those who excel around the greens. At Pinehurst, they had a distinct advantage inasmuch as everyone probably would struggle to hit greens in regulation.

"Pinehurst," Jaime Diaz wrote in *Sports Illustrated*, "is to chipping what Battle Creek is to cornflakes."

Chipping was deemed so important that players focused their practice rounds around the greenside shots. When Payne Stewart missed the cut at the FedEx St. Jude Classic the Friday before, he went straight to Pinehurst and spent the weekend walking the course and practicing only shots around and on the greens. He experimented with everything from a two-iron through a lob wedge in an effort to determine the best method to attack shots from the swales and hollows around the green. Several players employed the three-wood chip, an old-time shot that essentially had been resurrected by Tiger Woods. "You have so many options," Woods said, "that you can actually get kind of confused. It brings out imagination."

The most popular play, considering how short the USGA had moved the fringe and slope areas, would become the Texas wedge, the putter from off the green. The players would roll the ball up the rather steep slopes and onto the greens. The favorites to win were those capable of mastering the shots from around these greens, inasmuch as they were certain to encounter a plethora of them.

Native North Carolinians call them turtleback greens, and though they are relatively large and appear to be an inviting target from the fairway, the slopes reduce the effective putting surface to about 40 percent of the green. Miss that 40 percent from the fairway and the ball won't stay on the green.

"This mounding makes possible an infinite variety of nasty short shots that no other form of hazard can call for," Donald Ross wrote.

After the '99 Open at Pinehurst, David Duval was afforded the opportunity to take batting practice with the New York Mets, inspiring this analogy of Pinehurst's crowned greens: "I told them it was like trying to stop a six-iron on the pitcher's mound."

Paul Azinger won the Tour Championship at Pinehurst in 1992 and had this assessment: "I've never played Pine Valley, but this is as tough as I've seen. Take the ball down low, take it up high. Chip the ball with your sand wedge, your seven-iron. Pitch off a tight lie. Putt from off the green. It's just really hard. This is the way golf was meant to be played."

The USGA also appeased (probably unwittingly) those who often criticized it for taking the driver out of play in the U.S. Open, by its annual exercise of growing the rough and narrowing the fairways. This requires players to do whatever is required of them to ensure they keep the ball in play, usually by hitting a fairway wood or long iron from the tee. This time, the fairways were generous, by Open standards, inviting more aggressive play from the tees.

"I do feel more relaxed when I stand on the first tee here," Phil Mickelson said. "I feel like I don't have to be perfect. I don't feel like there are red stakes lining each fairway, as I have felt in past Opens. I feel like a slight error, there's still an opportunity for recovery. It's a very fair test. The rough isn't ridiculous."

Jack Nicklaus came through on behalf of the field, when he toured the course before the Open and suggested the rough be trimmed an inch, from four inches to three. The USGA agreed.

"This is definitely an atypical U.S. Open setup," USGA executive director David Fay said. "If I had to voice one inside-the-ropes concern, it's that we have to be careful not to allow the rough to get away from us so it becomes the pitch-out variety. If the greens remain firm and fast, it's going to look like a pinball machine. It's prudent to start at four inches and maybe trim back four or five days before."

So there was the setup: wider than normal fairways, lower than normal rough, and greens adroit at the goal-line stand. The greens were the course's defense, protecting the integrity of par, unless those who routinely work magic around the green were capable of solving the riddle.

That was the pretournament consensus: that the course favored the short-game magicians, Phil Mickelson and Masters champion Jose Maria Olazabal among them. The theory wavered early; Olazabal opened with a 75 that he did not accept with any degree of poise. He attempted to vent by engaging a wall in a fight. The wall won, as it usually does in such encounters; Olazabal punched it and broke a bone in his hand, forcing him to withdraw.

"I'd say it sounds like he misclubbed himself," Greg Norman said. "It's always smarter to kick than punch."

The Open at Pinehurst played out the way one would hope, even the USGA, by sifting out most of the debris that does not belong on a major championship leaderboard, leaving only marquee players wrestling one another down the stretch. David Duval and Phil Mickelson were part of a group of four tied for the lead after the first round. Stewart, Duval, and Mickelson were tied after two.

The third round was the toughest of the tournament and the second most difficult round at an open in the '90s, behind only the final round of the '92 Open at Pebble Beach. John Cook was in the first pairing out in the morning and jokingly said he played it as a par 88. So he shot an eleven-under par 77, by his reckoning. "A birdie today is out of the question unless you chip in, hole a bunker shot, or make a thirty-foot putt," he said. "You're not going to hit it close from anywhere on the fairway."

When Cook and his playing partner, Miguel Angel Jiminez, finished their round, Jiminez said, "Thanks for the game. I enjoyed it."

"You liar," Cook replied, smiling.

The scoring average was 75.97, surprisingly high, considering the weather did not aggressively intervene. The breeze was moderate, reaching maybe fifteen miles per hour. The difference was that the cement from which the greens ostensibly were constructed hardened, leaving incoming shots without brakes. In fact, it hadn't rained since early in the week, and the course dried out.

"These putting surfaces . . . remind me of college," wrote *Golf World*'s Bob Verdi. "It's one thing to get there, but it's another thing to stay there."

Jack Nicklaus likened an attempt at hitting a green with "trying to stop a ball on the hood of a Volkswagen."

Hal Sutton, who ranked second on the PGA Tour in greens in regulation to that point, hit only 40 of 72 greens in regulation, 56 percent, more than 14 percent below his average entering the tournament.

One player, Bob Burns, went eighteen consecutive holes without hitting a green in regulation, the back nine on Friday and the front nine on Saturday.

Tiger Woods said he hit a lot of greens. "The ball didn't stay on them, but I hit them," he said.

Lee Janzen, who won the Open on an exceedingly difficult Olympic Club course a year earlier, said, "I've been asked many times to name the hardest course I've ever played," he said. "Now I have the answer."

Brandel Chamblee called it Augusta on steroids. *Golf World* called it the Pillage in the Village and Pinehearse No. 2.

"Obviously, we don't like seeing the best players in the world shoot high scores," said the USGA's Tom Meeks, who set up the course, "but when the wind kicks up, it's not like we can flick off a switch."

Those with a chance to win on Sunday represented a vast cross section of the game's best players, including Woods, Mickelson, Stewart, Duval, Vijay Singh, Sutton. The next wave included Davis Love, Justin Leonard, Montgomerie, Jesper Parnevik.

At the opposite end of the leaderboard was the inimitable John Daly, who is long on talent, longer off the tee, and commensurately short in patience. He once took an 18 at the Bay Hill Classic by hitting 5 straight balls into the water in a *Tin Cup* attempt at clearing the water with a three-wood. Daly had begun the '99 Open with a 68 and declared himself smitten with the course. By Sunday afternoon, Daly had begun divorce proceedings, citing irreconcilable differences. His tank of patience on empty, he missed the eighth green long and attempted to putt his ball up the slope and toward the hole. He failed to hit it hard enough, however, and the ball retreated toward him. "Donald [Ross] got him," as the locals like to say of such foiled efforts.

He attempted another similar putt and this one, too, lacked the requisite power and it also started rolling back toward him. Donald got him again. Donald had also discovered his breaking point. A disgusted Daly swung his putter at the moving ball and belted it on and over the green, incurring a two-stroke penalty, two of eleven strokes he needed to complete that hole. He wound up shooting an 83.

"It's not worth it," Daly said, launching into one of his better harangues. "This is my last U.S. Open, ever. I've had it with the USGA and the way they run their tournaments. The USGA loves to embarrass guys who play in their tournaments. I don't mind hitting the ball bad, but when I feel like I've hit the ball pretty good for four days and shoot an 81, it's not golf. It's crazy. My hat's off to whoever wins, and it's a major, but I don't consider the U.S. Open a major anymore. The U.S. Open is not John Daly's style of golf. I think the courses are set up unfair. I'm not going to Pebble Beach [for the 2000 Open] and see the USGA ruin that golf course as well."

The following day, Daly hand wrote a letter of apology to USGA executive director David Fay. In it, he said, "While I have some problems with the way the USGA sets up courses at the Open, it was wrong for me to talk about them the way that I did, and I regret my behavior."

This may have been true, but it turned out that Daly authored the letter of apology at the urging of Callaway Golf, his benefactor at the time.

"We accept his apology and look forward to seeing him at Pebble Beach," Fay said.

Fay later said that from his standpoint Daly's actions on the eighth hole spoke louder than his derogatory words that explained them. "The thing I'm worried about is that it might be a trend," Fay said, recalling that Kirk Triplett was guilty of a similar act on the eighteenth green at the Olympic Club in the Open the year before.

Daly was not the only infantile concern that week. The subplot unfolding over the course of the week was Amy Mickelson's pregnancy. She was not due for about two weeks and was home in Scottsdale, Arizona, but husband Phil was in possession of a beeper, had a private jet standing by, and was prepared to abandon his bid at winning his first major, were the call to come. He vowed he would unhesitatingly leave, even were he in the lead and on the brink of victory.

Amy revealed later that her first contractions came on Saturday evening, hours after the completion of the third round, with Mickelson trailing Payne Stewart by only a stroke. She went to the hospital and was given Tribulatin, a drug developed to slow the labor process. Meanwhile, she refrained from beeping her husband.

Throughout play on Sunday, Mickelson was in contention and the beeper stayed silent. The USGA could not have known, of course, but it might have been doing Mickelson a favor by telling him and Stewart to pick up the pace.

Slow play is the bane of golf, either for the amateur at home or the professional on tour, and on the latter front, officials have attempted to alleviate the problem by closely monitoring it. Each of the final two groups on Sunday at Pinehurst received slow-play warnings. First were Tiger Woods and Tim Herron, on the eighth hole. They picked up their pace, leaving a gap between them and Stewart and Mickelson, who were warned on the twelfth hole. A second warning would have carried with it a one-stroke penalty.

"It's the last group of the U.S. Open," Stewart said to the USGA official. "I didn't know it was a track meet."

Woods, in the penultimate group, concurred. "I disagree with being timed when you're in the last few groups of a major championship," he said. "If the greens are flat, fine, put us on the clock. But if they're severe, it takes time to figure out the slopes. If I understand the pace of play rule, there are [supposed to be exceptions]. Looking at these greens, I think they're a pretty good exception."

When it is a player's turn to hit, he has forty seconds to prepare himself and to execute the shot. "Some of these shots you face here are not forty-second shots," Brandel Chamblee said. "They're minute-and-a-half shots."

Tom Meeks of the USGA explained that the rules are clear and they're the same for everyone in the field, whether they're first off or last off. "I'll say this," Meeks said, "they responded. They got back in position and I left them alone. In my opinion, if we don't tell them, they're not going to make an effort."

Late in the final round, Mickelson concluded that he was probably going to win, providing him a wonderful story to tell his daughter one day. He was 1 stroke ahead of Stewart through fifteen holes and Stewart had a twenty-five-foot par putt, while Mickelson an eight-footer for par, creating the potential for increasing his lead to two strokes over Stewart and one over Woods. "At that moment," Mickelson said a year later, "I thought it was between Tiger and myself."

Instead, it was a two-shot swing in the wrong direction, Stewart holing his putt and Mickelson missing his. They were now tied. *Golf*

World later called Stewart's improbable par putt "the turning point in one of the most riveting nine-hole stretches in U.S. Open history."

Ahead of them, Woods nearly holed a bunker shot, but missed a short par putt and bogeyed the seventeenth hole, returning the focus to Stewart and Mickelson.

At hole seventeen, Stewart hit his approach shot to three feet of the hole, in the process changing Mickelson's assessment of the situation. "As soon as Payne hit that ball on seventeen, that was the first time I realized he could beat me." When Mickelson missed his birdie putt and Stewart made his, the latter had a one-stroke lead.

Stewart hit a poor drive from the eighteenth tee, the ball catching a rotten lie in the rough, giving him no choice other than to lay up short of the green. He now had seventy-seven yards to the pin and two shots to win the Open. His lob wedge third shot was pedestrian, leaving him staring at twenty feet that at that moment surely resembled twenty miles. He lined up the putt and remembered his wife Tracey's troubleshooting tip—that he'd been moving his head on putts. He stroked the putt and did not look up until it was about two feet from the hole.

"I can't describe the feeling that was going through my body when I looked up and saw that putt going into the hole," Stewart said. The ball fell into the cup, the longest putt ever made to win the Open on the seventy-second hole. "I couldn't believe my eyes."

Stewart won with an exhibition of putting more familiar to an audience of the Bob Hope Chrysler Classic than the U.S. Open. He needed only twenty-four putts in the final round. "I putted my little derriere off today," Stewart said.

Stewart was the only player in the field to play seventy-two holes under par, and by only one-under par at that.

As for Mickelson, he returned home that night and his wife's water broke at 9 A.M. on Monday, at precisely the time Mickelson would have been arriving at the first tee for a play-off, had there been one. Amanda Mickelson entered the world a few hours later.

The 1999 U.S. Open would be remembered for Stewart's victory, his last (he died in an airplane incident four months later), and for the Mickelson family drama, but its imprimatur was that the USGA had reintroduced driving and chipping back into the equation, and that Pinehurst had performed splendidly, surely muscling its way into the Open rotation.

"So many things came back into style during the 99th U.S. Open that one half expected to be able to buy a Coke for a dime or watch Sam Snead putt for birdie before the week was through," Bill Fields wrote in *Golf World*. "Hitting driver off the tee was back. Chipping and putting were back. Imagination was back. Most of all, the No. 2 Course, long revered but only once utilized as the site of a professional major, was back. It was a layout at once frustrating and refreshing, penalizing yet fair; these factors prevented attrition from pushing aside drama, as is so often the case in a U.S. Open."

Even the loser was generous with his praise. "I think this is the best test of golf I've ever played in a major championship," Mickelson said. "It tests every shot."

It was, ironically, the kind of Open that Seve Ballesteros might have won, had it been played fifteen years earlier, before his game took a leave of absence and never bothered to return. He would have been permitted to drive it crooked occasionally, and his sleight of hand around the greens would have begged the question: How'd he do that?

Then again, it would have run counter to what the USGA ostensibly asks of Open participants: that they leave their most lethal weapons at home and wage war without them. It's better that Ballesteros was never introduced to Pinehurst, then, lest the battlefield chosen by the USGA be forced to surrender for once.

The possibility that an Open course would yield to a player's skill in defiance of an historical pattern was anathema to the USGA, which only a year later stood by and helplessly watched an Open course succumb.

15

A WALK ON THE BEACH

PEBBLE BEACH GOLF LINKS, 2000

The infiltration of new money into Pebble Beach became apparent when a man paid $10 million for a French country estate along 17 Mile Drive and christened his new quarters *Dot Calm*.

Newly minted multimillionaires (and billionaires) searching for second homes inevitably would look to Pebble Beach and Carmel, only about a ninety-minute drive from the Silicon Valley—that noted agricultural hotbed where for a while they were growing money on trees. As weekend retreats for the nouveau riche of northern California dot com lineage go, the Monterey Peninsula is preferable to, say, Oakland or Stockton.

The influx of new money into Pebble Beach, its own home-away-from-home, was not an unwelcome occurrence for the USGA, even as it historically had established a preference for old money. This was a position it had expediently come to regard as passé by 2000, when at its annual meeting in January, the organization reported assets of $170 million. The USGA was flush from savvy investing that included timely buys in the technology sector.

New money or old, it now might have asked dismissively, What's the difference?

This could have been interpreted as a sign that the once-rigid USGA was using less starch these days. Another was that only a year before at Pinehurst, it had allowed players to wield their drivers in the U.S. Open, without having to post a warning, *Use at your own risk.* Even more telling was the fact that it had ordered the rough for the 2000 Open at Pebble Beach not to exceed three inches, a benevolent gesture that suggested that mulligans and gimmes were in the offing.

Even the decision to return to Pebble Beach in 2000, only eight years after it was last played there, was an anomaly. The last time an Open had returned to a venue as few as eight years later was 1935, when it went back to Oakmont, site of the '27 Open. Pebble Beach had been on a ten-year rotation, but the impending pseudomillennium, in conjunction with the centennial U.S. Open, begged that the cathedral of American golf host the Open in this landmark year, just as the Royal and Ancient elected to take the British Open to the birthplace of golf, St. Andrews, later in the summer of 2000.

"The one-hundredth playing of the United States Open, right here at Pebble Beach, is about as close to perfection as you can get," USGA president Dr. Trey Holland said.

It was the fourth time since 1972 that the USGA had brought the Open to Pebble Beach, the most popular Open venue over a four-decade span. The USGA was smitten; its pulse raced in the company of Pebble Beach, nearly eradicating all uncertainty over whether it actually had a heart.

The existence of a heart officially was verified by the coronary the

USGA nearly suffered when it learned that the three-inch rough was more ally than enemy to the players. Mike Davis, the USGA man on site at Pebble, recognized the problem and relayed his concerns to Tom Meeks, the USGA director of rules and competitions. Johnny Miller and Roger Maltbie—NBC golf analysts who had ventured down from their northern California homes a few weeks before the Open to play the course—also recognized that the three-inch rough was more merciful than merciless. They also phoned the USGA with their concerns.

"I don't know what happened between our visit here at the end of April and at the end of May," Meeks said. "In a perfect world, we wanted to have three inches of rough. That's what we had last year at Pinehurst, and we thought that was one of our best courses. But at three inches of rough here, the ball was sitting up like it was on a tee."

It presented a quandary only in a superficial sense. Given a choice between a course playing easier or harder, there was no choice. The USGA shed its kinder, gentler masquerade and reacted predictably: Rather than allowing the course to take a beating, it opted to let the players take a beating. The decision was made that the rough would be grown at least another inch to an inch and a half, which proved the difference between it being friend or foe.

So, when the players arrived, they encountered typical Open rough. One of them called the efforts required to muscle the ball out of the rough and back to the safety of the fairway "hack-gouge shots." Nick Price said the rough "is so matted and so thick you might never get the thing out."

"At three, three and a half inches, it didn't bring out the half-shot penalty we like to see," said Tim Moraghan, the USGA's championship agronomist. "So we set it at four, four-and-a-half inches. It is dense. It is thick. You have to remember that at one time, what is now the four to eight yards of primary rough inside the ropes for the players was once fairway. So the density is a little thicker. The grass is a little tighter. Once it gets up around four inches, it's going to be hard to get the ball out. We're going to have a variety of shots. Some that disappear, some that get half-buried, others sitting up. It's the luck of the draw. And, you know, you're supposed to hit in the fairways, anyway."

Phil Mickelson, who welcomed the opportunity a year earlier to exhibit his superiority at chipping the ball, railed against the USGA decision to heighten the rough, in effect taking chipping out of the game and replacing it with something requiring conspicuously less skill.

"We are not being tested in every area of the game," he said. "We have been asked to create unskilled shots. Hacking out to forty feet [of the hole] isn't skillful. Three-inch rough would have allowed for skilled chipping, but the problem for the USGA is that the ball sits on top when the grass is that length. And when it's five inches, the ball sinks to the bottom."

Jack Nicklaus weighed in and suggested that the rough was more penalizing than the USGA might have wanted it. "The rough is very thick right now," he said.

Swedish star Jesper Parnevik said, "It's playing tougher than I thought. That rough doesn't look like much, but it's probably one of the thickest roughs we've had in any U.S. Open lately."

A proponent of less rough at Pebble Beach again was Grant Spaeth, the former USGA president and a Pebble Beach expert. Once more, he suggested that the rough along the right side of the seaside holes—four, six, and eight through ten—be eliminated and replaced with hard, fast fairway incapable of stopping a wayward shot before it tumbled off the end of the cliff, as it has played since Spaeth first went there as a kid. Spaeth was of the opinion that it might have made the course even harder. The USGA rejected his suggestion.

The rough was not the USGA's only effort at arming the course. It also had resurfaced the greens in concrete (figuratively, of course). "The U.S. Open has always been about playing a firm, fast course with a rough that provides a subtle penalty," Meeks said. Of course, a subtle penalty by USGA standards requires search parties to rescue those who have strayed into the rough and can't find their way out.

The USGA's infatuation with Pebble Beach extends beyond mere beauty. It appreciates the course's feistiness, with or without its assistance. "It doesn't look like a course that's going to kill you," Tom Watson said, "but before you know it it does." The primary weapon Pebble Beach uses is the wind, which has always been an ally for the USGA's. It recognized the wind's value in a way similar to how famed architect C. B. Macdonald so eloquently expressed his appreciation for it. "Wind," Macdonald said, "I consider the finest asset in golf. In itself it is one of the greatest and most delightful accompaniments in the game. Without wind your course is always the same, but as the wind varies in velocity and from the various points of the compass, you not only have one course but you have many courses."

The USGA also recognized wind as a convenient target toward which it could deflect blame, in the event the course became an unplayable lie, as it did in the final round in both 1972 and 1992.

The USGA feigned surprise that the wind had so forcefully intruded on its Open championship in those years. On the sincerity scale, this does not even minutely move the needle. Pebble Beach is a seaside course, *seaside* being the operative word here. The surprise would be, if nature were to develop a beach at which the wind does not blow.

"Personally, I hope we get some wind," Meeks said, as though it was not a given. "If you don't have some wind, Pebble Beach is almost defenseless. I don't want gales, but some good, healthy wind each day."

Among the trickiest holes in the wind would be the new par-3 fifth, designed by Jack Nicklaus and placing the hole where it ought to have gone in the first place—along the cliff overlooking Stillwater Cove and filling in the gap of seaside holes, now running from the fourth through the tenth, before returning again at seventeen. When Samuel Morse had the course built, the land on which the new fifth was constructed was not available, so a shorter, uphill, inland par 3, sheltered from the stronger winds, was built. Eventually, survivors of the original owners of the seaside plot that had eluded Morse decided to sell, enabling a new fifth to be built on land that he had coveted for that purpose.

"I like the hole," Tiger Woods said during the AT&T Pebble Beach National Pro-Am earlier in the year. "But I think if we get a strong wind into our faces on the tee, we could literally hit a wood on the hole. And it would be very interesting."

When Nicklaus visited the course in January, he noticed that rough was being grown in the bailout area left of the green, contrary to how he had designed it, and that it had been done at the behest of the USGA. "Guys, that's not supposed to be rough," Nicklaus told USGA officials. "You need fairway to the left of the green. If you miss on that side, you need to be able to chip the ball. You need to bounce it. That won't be possible if there is rough right down to the green. That's not how the hole was designed. I shaped the hole so that the fairway feeds down to the hole from the left. If you miss the green in the rough, you've then got a place to bounce the ball into the hole."

Did the USGA listen? "Nicklaus was wasting his breath," *Golf World* wrote. "The apparently omniscient USGA—as it so often does—ignored the advice of the greatest golfer ever. When the best players in the game arrived . . . at Pebble Beach for the 100th U.S. Open, they found long grass growing within a few feet of every putting surface, the fifth included."

Nicklaus also was among those who protested the USGA turning the par-5 second hole into a par 4, reducing par for the course to 71 for the first time in four Opens played there. His voice was only one in a chorus of them. Players generally do not appreciate the USGA altering par on a hole. "I would argue that if you select a great course to host your tournament, then you should respect its greatness," Peter Jacobsen wrote in his book *Buried Lies: True Tales and Tall Stories from the PGA Tour*. "Making those changes is like hosting an art show and saying, 'For this special show, we're going to turn Leonardo Da Vinci's *Last*

Supper into a Texas barbecue, and add one arm to the Venus de Milo, so she can embellish the product of our corporate sponsor, Rolex.' "

Tiger Woods was among those weighing in against the USGA. "Why change something when you have such a historical reference?" Woods said. "We've always played this golf course as a par 72. We've had major championships on this course, and all of a sudden it's a par 71. I don't think that's right, because you can't compare the shots to the ones the champions of past years made.

"When you shoot 284, that should be four under. Now it's even par."

So what? This is the USGA's general response to such criticism. As former executive director Frank Hannigan said, "Suppose you called it a par 6? What difference does it make? A lot of them have never figured out that they're not playing the USGA, they're playing each other. The low score is going to win, no matter what the relation to par is. Par is of interest just because it gives us a way of keeping score in relative terms on television."

The counter to Hannigan's position would be, Then why bother? The only logical conclusion is that the USGA does it as a psychological ploy, providing the players with another reason to bemoan the difficulty of the course.

The USGA's official response was delivered by executive committee member Fred Ridley, who pointed out that in the U.S. Amateur there the summer before, the hole was also played as a par 4. Most players hit four- or five-iron into the green with their second shots now that the danger, the old, dying Monterey pines that protected the green, had finally succumbed to pitch canker disease. "So from that standpoint," Ridley said, "we felt it was an appropriate test for that hole to play as a par 4."

Phil Mickelson reasoned that changing a number is a better solution to protecting the integrity of par than what the USGA more often does. "It's one of the best golf courses in the world, created many, many years ago," Mickelson said. "I'm not a big fan of altering it. But I'd rather see them do that to keep scores around par than do some of the other things I've seen them do, as far as making greens hard as a brick and not being able to hold a shot, even with a perfect wedge from the fairway. I'd rather see them just change par on paper."

The USGA is no paper tiger, however. It wants more from a course than simple intimidation, and it got it from Pebble Beach. "Most guys say they ruin Pebble Beach by what they do to it at a U.S. Open," Tiger Woods said. "Unfortunately, they make it very hard, very severe, and those greens aren't designed for that. They're designed for a little softer condition."

Fog is a softener, certainly, by dampening the turf and slowing it down, and by keeping the wind in check. The first round of the 2000 Open was marred by fog, though not before Tiger Woods had finished a flawless round of six-under par 65 that gave him a one-stroke lead over a man who failed to grasp the enormity of the story unfolding in his midst.

Woods had dominated golf in the fifteen months leading to the Open. He won eight tournaments in 1999, including the PGA Championship, and he had already won four times in 2000. He had turned professional golf into the Tiger Woods Show, relegating anything else that happened in golf to a supporting role.

Miguel Angel Jiminez, the Spaniard who opened with a 66, was dissatisfied with the role. "I'm tired of this," he said in response to a question about Woods. "Tiger is the best player in the world, but you'd think there's only one player here. There are one hundred fifty-six of the best players in the world here."

One hundred fifty-five by the time the inimitable John Daly had completed his first round. Daly, having reneged on his promise a year earlier never to play in the Open again, made a mockery of his return engagement, a single mistake detonating his exceedingly short fuse. He arrived at the eighteenth tee of the first round having put together a respectable score to that point, then hit his tee shot out of bounds right. He reloaded and hooked his next into the water, then duplicated the shot. He pulled a five-iron for his next effort, simply to keep the ball in play.

He laid up with his next shot, leaving him 115 yards to the green, a relatively simple shot on the professional level. Instead, he put that one in the water, too. He took a drop in a bunker, the ball settling next to a sea wall, requiring that he play the next shot left-handed. He left that one in the bunker. He finally blasted his ball onto the green and took two putts, then summoned an accountant, or probably should have. All told, he was assessed fourteen strokes and finished with an 83.

After signing his scorecard, he withdrew from the tournament and departed the premises without saying anything other than, "Get me to the airport fast."

His caddie was former NHL player Dan Quinn, who was left to answer for him. "It's amazing how quickly it went," Quinn said. "He just got all beat up at the end. One little swing and it was like, 'Oh, my God.' I feel bad for the kid. He's a great guy. He's so talented."

The fog postponed the end of the first round to Friday morning and the end of the second round to Saturday morning, at which time it was apparent to everyone, even Jiminez, that this was a one-man show. Woods opened a six-shot lead, despite making a bogey on the eighteenth hole of round two, triggering an impromptu analysis that provided more insight into his unique wiring than he ever volunteers.

Woods snapped his tee shot there into the ocean, then whirled and slammed his club into the turf, his choreography accompanied by a few choice words: "Goddammit, you fucking prick!"

The ubiquitous boom mike was nearby and his commentary came across the national airwaves loud and clear, early on a Saturday morning, no less—cartoon hour across much of the country. "I'm one of those guys who plays pretty intense," Woods said, "and unfortunately I let it slip out. And I regret doing it. But unfortunately it happened."

It was a display that appropriately earned him widespread condemnation, but it also provided a glimpse of what his de facto pursuit is, and it isn't Nicklaus's record. Woods's goal is perfection, unattainable in this game, a fact that won't discourage him from trying, and a shot that fell woefully short of perfect, even as he was stretching his lead, was sufficient to set off an explosion.

By the end of the second round, only three players stood under par: Woods at eight under; Jiminez at two under; and Jose Maria Olazabal at one under.

The fifth hole contributed its share to the wretched scoring by playing as Nicklaus had predicted it would. When Australian Paul Gow bogeyed the hole en route to a 79 in the first round and left the green, he was overheard muttering to himself, "Horrendous golf course."

The USGA had diminished the quality of the hole by removing any margin for error. The players needed to guard against hitting it right, where the cliff and the cove waited to dispense punishment. But a miss left was not a palatable alternative, either, given the rough the USGA had ordered.

"Everybody is missing the green left," Nicklaus said, "and nobody has a shot, nobody can make par. You've got the cliff on one side and no shot whatsoever if you miss it left."

Nicklaus questioned the wisdom of taking "the smile off the Mona Lisa." John Cook simply called the hole a nightmare.

The wind amplified the difficulty of the hole, creating a logjam in the process, with as many as three groups on the tee at once. A pair of USGA officials wondered aloud why the hole was playing so slow.

"It's because you guys won't let it be played the way it was designed," Nicklaus said to them.

The bumpy poa annua greens were another nuisance for the players. They become more difficult to putt when they are cropped short, preventing golfers from putting a firm stroke on a putt to keep it on line. A firm stroke and a missed putt on a perilously fast green spell doom.

"Worst greens I've ever putted on," John Huston said on Saturday, in stark contrast to what he said after opening the tournament with a 67. Then, he said the greens were perfect.

"No question about it," he said after a round of 76. "They're so bumpy, they're dead. It's pot luck where the ball's going to roll. You can't step up and say, 'I'm going to hit a good putt just outside the left' and know it's going to break where it should. It's just terrible."

Huston claimed he played better in shooting 76 than he had in shooting 67 in the first round. "It's unbelievable," he said. "You just have to laugh at it and hope for the best. I just don't understand it."

Saturday was no fun for anyone other than the leader, Woods, who shot an even-par 71 to increase his lead from 6 shots to 10. The wind gave a command performance in the afternoon, further drying out hard greens thirsting for water, and even began to turn them brown.

"I'm embarrassed," said Hale Irwin, a three-time U.S. Open champion who shot 81. "I'm humiliated. I got my big dose of humble pie today."

Irwin was one of sixteen players from a field of sixty-three—better than one in four—to fail to break 80. Jim Furyk, among the better, more consistent players on the PGA Tour, shot an 84.

The scoring average on Saturday was 77.12, only a tick better than it had been in the final round of the '92 Open at Pebble Beach, one of the more difficult days in U.S. Open history. The par-4 eighth and ninth holes nearly played as par 5s, their stroke average 4.825. The field collectively failed to hit half the greens in regulation, a dismal performance, by tour standards.

Ernie Els, one of only three players to equal or better par, shot a 68 that he called "the best 68 I ever shot," and was the only player to gain ground on Woods.

Tom Lehman shot a 78 which he gracefully accepted. "You had to play well to shoot a good score," he said. "If you weren't playing good golf, the course just ate you alive today. And that's really the way it should be. It separated the guys who have their games today from the guys who didn't."

Even Woods succumbed to the difficulty of the course, however briefly. On the third hole, he hit his second shot short and right, into thick rough by the green. His first swing failed to dislodge the ball. To ensure his escape, he came out sideways with his next stroke, then chipped on and took two putts. It added to a triple-bogey 7 that reduced his lead from eight shots to five, yet the temper tantrum of which he is capable failed to materialize. Woods merely smiled wryly, then went about his business.

"I felt very, very calm inside, even when I made triple," Woods said. "I felt the same way when I won at Augusta."

The winner had already been determined, barring an injury. "It's not like boxing where you give a guy a low blow," Paul Azinger said. "We might need Tonya Harding or something."

The final round was a victory lap for Woods, who on another difficult day did not make a bogey and shot 67, to win by an astonishing 15 strokes. Woods finished seventy-two holes in twelve-under par 272, sending the record book back to its editor for wholesale changes.

Only one player previously had ever gotten to double figures under par—Dr. Gil Morgan, at the '92 Open at Pebble—and he finished at five-over par. Woods became the second, only he was loath to back pedal. His score of 272 tied Jack Nicklaus and Lee Janzen for the Open record for fewest strokes, while the twelve-under shattered the record of eight-under held jointly by Ben Hogan, Jack Nicklaus, and Lee Janzen.

The margin of victory was the largest in major championship history, erasing a record that had stood since Old Tom Morris won the British Open by 13 strokes in 1862. Another ancient record to fall was for margin of victory in a U.S. Open, the old mark of 11 set by Willie Smith in 1899.

"I'm definitely mortal," Rocco Mediate said. "I think we all are. But Tiger's not. He's just better in all aspects of the game, especially mentally."

Pebble Beach was a miserable, angry golf course that might have gotten buried beneath an avalanche of criticism had Woods not rendered all such complaints immaterial. How excessively difficult could the course have been if the winner established an Open record in relation to par?

The question is an unfair one. Woods's performance gave rise to the notion that golf had never before been introduced to a player with skills of this magnitude; that even the old man taking his final Open bows, at the eighteenth hole of the second round, failed to exhibit skills that sufficiently matched up.

Jack Nicklaus, now sixty, had played in the Open for the last time, shooting his highest Open score ever, an 82, in his final Open round. "Hard and fast were my favorite conditions," he said. "That's when I excelled. Now I can't make those conditions work."

They worked wonderfully for the first man ever to fulfill the role of Bear Apparent, the next Nicklaus. In winning for the first time a tournament Nicklaus had won four times, Woods had pieced together the Open's equivalent of a perfect game. "If that's not perfect," said Els, who tied for second, "I don't know what is. Just a perfect display of golf. If you want to watch a guy win the U.S. Open playing perfectly, you've just seen it."

Among the contributing factors to Woods's prowess is that he was not viewing his own performance in a similar vein. His teacher, Butch Harmon, related a conversation he'd had with Woods on Saturday night. "He's got a ten-shot lead," Harmon said, "and he wants to know what's wrong with his swing, why is he hitting so many loose irons."

The irony is that had it been possible to remove Woods from the story line, one of the more difficult Opens in history would have been left behind, resulting in another knockout victory for Pebble Beach. Els and Jiminez tied for second at three-over par, a score more in line with what the USGA would have preferred.

Pebble Beach held its own against an onslaught of players, but it was rendered defenseless by a solitary star disinclined to follow the USGA script that calls for the golf course to win in the end.

16

THE MUNY

BLACK COURSE AT BETHPAGE STATE PARK, 2001

Egalitarian was a word over which the otherwise erudite and eloquent members of the USGA executive committee routinely tripped over the years, as though it were foreign to them or an epithet that was not suitable for use in polite company.

Evidence suggests it was both. This was their reputation, at least, and it was not necessarily unfounded. A cursory check of the committee members over the years would have turned up no truck drivers, no assembly-line workers, no bricklayers, no store clerks, no bank tellers, no teachers.

Their club affiliations, meanwhile, seemed as though they were taken straight from *Golf Digest*'s biennial feature, *America's 100 Greatest*

Golf Courses, starting not near the bottom of the list, either, but at or near the top: Pine Valley, Merion, Seminole, Winged Foot, Oakmont.

Until 1972, the USGA had not condescended to taking the Open to a course at which the *public* (gasp!) was welcome, and then it did so only reluctantly and with trepidation. At that, Pebble Beach, though a public facility, has always been more closely aligned with the privileged than the underprivileged, or even the middle class, as the humorist and neophyte golfer Bill Geist noted in the *New York Times*. "People dressed to mow the lawn don't show up to play golf at Pebble Beach," he wrote. "They do at most public courses."

The USGA's history of taking the Open to courses to which the public has access is as thin as the excuse it once used for neglecting to do so. Those arguing against taking the Open to Pebble Beach in 1972, for instance, cited the shallow pool of potential volunteers, inasmuch as there was no membership from which to draw. They also noted the inability to keep a tight rein on those playing the course in the months leading to the Open, the way it was able to restrain members at private clubs.

The Open, heretofore, has been played on only two courses open to the public, Pebble Beach and the No. 2 Course at Pinehurst, and neither is particularly accessible to the masses. Each is part of a resort with a stringent dress code: Deep pockets required. The cost of a green fee at either is more than $300. Moreover, access is limited unless the golfer is a guest of the respective resort as well, requiring another considerable outlay.

Elitist is *not* a word on which members of the executive committee would trip. They wore it too comfortably throughout the years, even operating in a clandestine fashion that suggested that whatever it was they were up to, it was none of our business. "I've got a greater working knowledge of the Kennedy assassination than I do the USGA," Wally Uihlein, president and CEO of Titleist and FootJoy Worldwide, told *Golf World*. "It's as secretive as the CIA."

The self-anointed guardians of the game, a group instrumental in perpetuating the notion that golf is an elitist game, typically ignore their principal constituency, the public golf denizens, those who change their shoes in the parking lot, wear T-shirts or cutoff jeans as their golf attire, buy TopFlite XLs in fifteen-packs, carry ball retrievers, and own pull carts.

The vision of a single man, USGA executive director David Fay, dragged the USGA officials out from behind their guarded gates to address a pressing concern—the need to take the Open to a municipal course as the game was attempting to shed its elitist image and to reach out to the masses in earnest.

In May of 1995, Fay took a group that included colleagues from the USGA and prominent course architect Rees Jones out to play the Black Course at state-owned Bethpage State Park in Farmingdale, New York, in the woodlands of central Long Island, about an hour's drive from Manhattan. Bethpage features five courses on which 300,000 rounds are played each year and is the largest public-golf complex in the country.

Fay and his group went there to gauge whether the Black was a suitable site for a U.S. Open. It had the pedigree; it was designed by A. W. Tillinghast, a man who had Winged Foot and Baltusrol on his résumé, each of them Open sites, as well as an array of some of the world's most impressive courses.

One potential drawback was that the Black was untested as a tournament site on a high-profile stage. The New York State Open, the Metropolitan Open, the Long Island Open, and the Ivy League Championship have been held there, but no USGA, LPGA, or PGA Tour event had ever been played at Bethpage Black. The suggestion that the U.S. Amateur be played as a trial run for taking the Open there had been rejected.

Awarding the Open to a course without a form chart, from which it might handicap its opportunity to succeed, was contrary to USGA protocol and a risky venture. The PGA of America often gambled by awarding its PGA Championship to untested sites, with mixed results (Oak Tree in 1988, Kemper Lakes in 1989, Valhalla in 1996).

Still, Fay was enamored with this idea that had been percolating in his mind for many years. Twenty-seven years had passed since Fay last played Bethpage Black, as a high school student, and he had retained a thought that, were the Open ever to go to a true public facility, the Black was a viable candidate.

"We do a lot and say a lot about the importance of building more public golf courses," Fay said in 1995. "But holding the Open at a true public facility is something we've never done. Over half our member clubs are public in orientation. Pebble Beach and Pinehurst are the only two public courses we play our national championship on, but they're really resort courses. The whole idea is still in its infancy, but it's a dream of mine to hold the National Open at a place like Bethpage, which is the quintessential public facility."

When Fay and his group played there, the Black was in a state of disrepair, as are so many municipal courses. It was overplayed and undernourished, its superintendent staff undermanned. Trees evengrew from untended bunkers. Rees Jones, the younger son of the late architect Robert Trent Jones—and the man who inherited the mantle of Open doctor from his father—nonetheless recognized that beneath the grime was a gem that needed only some serious elbow grease.

"We came to the conclusion that the canvas was there," Jones said. "We just had to touch it up a little bit. It's a great piece of ground with great routing."

Rees Jones was so taken with the course and the cause that he volunteered his services to restore Bethpage Black in the event the USGA indeed decided to take the Open there.

Fay's own opinions of Bethpage Black were confirmed by others in the group as well. "I always thought that the Black Course was the symbol of public golf in this country," Fay told Newsday. "It was probably my first experience with what I thought was a great golf course. I don't know exactly when I first thought about it as an Open site, but when I did, I asked members of my staff to look at it and make sure I wasn't crazy. After they went and saw for themselves, they sort of vouched for my sanity."

More than a year later, on August 28, 1996, Fay and New York Governor George Pataki announced that the 2002 U.S. Open—*The People's Open*, as it would come to be called—would be played on the Black Course at Bethpage State Park, the first time the national championship was awarded to a publicly owned golf course.

"It's hard to overstate our enthusiasm for bringing our national championship to a golf course owned by the public," Fay said in a news release issued by Pataki's office. "Most courses and golfers today are public in orientation and this news just underscores how important public golf is to the game of golf."

The decision was immediately recognized as a winner from every perspective. The USGA was taking its marquee event onto the people's turf, to a course that at that time had a green fee of only $20 and still charges less than $40, possibly the best bargain in golf. The USGA was lowering its guard and venturing out among the commoners, a gesture of acknowledgment from the ruling body that golf indeed intended to transform itself into an egalitarian game.

"In the strict caste system of golf," Bill Geist wrote, "holding this celebrated golf tournament at a public course is nothing short of revolutionary, tantamount to holding a royal wedding at the Port Authority bus station."

The course, meanwhile, was in dire need of repairs for which the state could never have earmarked the necessary funds to bring it in line with Open requirements, and now it was relieved of the duty entirely. The USGA pledged $2.7 million to have the Black restored and assigned the task to Jones, accepting his offer to waive his fee. Jones called the course "one of Tillinghast's best," and recognized that its long par 4s and contoured greens were from the USGA's primer on Open courses.

Tillinghast in fact called Bethpage Black the Black Leopard because it "shows plenty of teeth." He also called it a mankiller. Those schooled in the nuances of the legends of course architecture recognize in Bethpage elements borrowed from Pine Valley, a George Crump and H. S. Colt design in New Jersey and widely regarded as one of the two or three best courses in the world. Rees Jones dubbed Bethpage Black "Tillinghast's Pine Valley."

Jones recalled Tillinghast's claim to have been involved in the design of a few holes at Pine Valley and noted similarities in the courses, including long, sandy wastelands and a fifth hole at the Black that closely resembles the sixteenth at Pine Valley.

Bethpage Black was essentially Tillinghast's parting gift to golf, one of the last courses he designed before leaving the business. Once a millionaire, Tillinghast had become a victim of the Depression and saw the bulk of his wealth evaporate. Bethpage in fact was an undertaking of the Works Project Administration, an agency designed to provide work on public projects during this period. Tillinghast designed three courses at Bethpage, but the Black was his crowning achievement there. It opened in 1936 and was instantly recognized as a formidable course of the highest quality.

The first requirement of an Open course is that it is of a sufficient quality, of course. Bethpage Black already had passed this test; it was ranked forty-sixth by *Golf Digest* in its latest biennial ranking of America's one-hundred greatest courses—not its first appearance on the list, incidentally. It was ranked one-hundredth in the 1997–1998 rankings, then dropped from the list in 1999–2000, as it was undergoing radical reconstructive surgery.

The second requirement is that the course can adequately counter players' skills and protect the integrity of par. By every account, the Black was sufficiently equipped to do so, even more than a half-century later. The layout is so difficult, by amateur standards, that the Black was once a course of last resort. Locals preferred to play the Red, Yellow, Blue, or Green at Bethpage, each of them considerably more forgiving of their three-piece swings and putting lunges. Only reluctantly would they venture over to play the Black and would do so usually only when they could not obtain a tee time on one of the other four courses.

Years ago, when waiting times for each of the courses was posted, it was not atypical to see, say, an hour's wait for the Red, thirty minutes for the Green, and zero minutes for the Black.

A sign at the first tee even warns the incurable slicer, the short hitter, the average golfer, to beware the Black, the way many Western United States courses alert golfers to the presence of rattlesnakes. In either case, exercise caution or you might get bit. The sign at the Black reads: "The Black course is an extremely difficult course which we recommend only to highly skilled golfers."

Another sign beside the first tee notes: "The last course ever designed by noted golf course architect A. W. Tillinghast, the championship Black Course was rated one of the most challenging in the country when it opened in the spring of 1936. The narrow fairways, severely contoured greens, numerous traps, and long carries combine with the natural topography to create a unique golfing experience not easily forgotten by its fans. One Bethpage golfer stationed in London during World War II wrote after the blitz, 'I've seen no bomb craters that I've studied as anxiously as I have the bunker guarding number 2 of the Black Course.' "

The effort to steer all but highly skilled golfers away from the Black has been a futile one of late. Once the USGA announced its intention to bring the Open to Bethpage Black, a course once largely ignored became the main attraction, providing the public a once-in-a-lifetime opportunity to play a bona fide U.S. Open course.

Jones's restoration included sharpening the teeth in Tillie's Black Leopard. Unable to locate the original blueprint, Jones employed an aerial photograph of the Black, taken in 1938 as a rudimentary blueprint for rebuilding the bunkers and greens to their original shapes. "It was not our Bible, but we used it as a guide," Rees Jones said. "We had to design in the context of today's player."

He stretched the course by more than three hundred yards to account for the distances the contemporary professionals are hitting the ball. The course is expected to play up to 7,300 yards and to a par of 70 for the Open.

"It's almost like we were looking into a crystal ball and saw players using solid balls," Jones said, noting that the restoration began before the advent of three-piece balls and 325-yard drives. "It is a modern championship layout, even though it's an old Tillinghast layout."

Small greens are its second line of defense against the contemporary player. "That's what's going to thwart the big hitters," Jones said. "Shrinking targets."

Jones's most radical change occurred at the par-4 eighteenth hole, which in its previous incarnation would not have been a suitable closer for an Open. The USGA expects the last hole of an Open to be capable of producing a dramatic finish, preferably by making it a difficult par rather than a relatively easy birdie, as the old eighteenth at the Black might have been, had it remained at 378 yards. The eighteenth is now the Black's signature hole.

"It was an easy, boring hole," said Jones, who stretched it to 420 yards, still short by modern dimensions. He borrowed a page from his father's primer, however, by expanding the fairway bunkers to a degree that they now pinch the landing area, dramatically reducing the margin for error. He also reduced by one third the size of the green, requiring a more precise second shot. He added another greenside bunker left of the green and brought closer a bunker to the right to better guard the green.

"It's a pretty formidable finishing hole," Jones said. "Four-twenty is the shortest par 4 on the back 9, but you're going to have to think your way through the hole."

A player attempting to make up a stroke on the seventy-second hole might choose to gamble by aiming for the narrow gap between the fairway bunkers, leaving him a shorter second shot. By doing so, he runs the risk of driving his ball into a bunker, dramatically hindering his effort at making birdie. The player who is one ahead might choose to lay his tee shot short of the fairway bunkers, leaving a longer, more difficult second shot to a guarded green. "One shot ahead or one behind," Jones said, "a lot can happen, especially if you hit it in one of the bunkers."

Four par 4s will measure greater than 480 yards, which, according to the USGA's abandoned protocols once outlined in the *Rules of Golf,* should make them par 5s. "I see some long par 4s down the road," said Tom Meeks, the USGA's director of rules and competitions, at the 2001 Open at Southern Hills, which featured the longest par 4 in Open history, 491 yards. "How much longer, I don't know."

The public won't have to play the Black from the back tees, obviously, but even from forward tees it still will provide a representative test and one that will allow paying customers to experience an Open-quality course. The fact that Bethpage has four other courses, each of them easier, gave Jones carte blanche to ensure that the Black was a ferocious course.

"Bethpage is like a major ski resort," Jones said. "You can go to a black diamond slope or you can go to a green slope. The public golfers can test themselves for one day on the Black, and then go back to more familiar surroundings the next day. The fact that the Black is one of five courses at their facility gave us the opportunity to realize one of Tillinghast's ultimate tests."

Once the Open is gone, the public golfers in New York State will have an authentic A. W. Tillinghast U.S. Open course to call their own. "It really is a gift to the game, from the state of New York," Jones said. "We're embracing a whole new element of player and showing them that they're now part of golf in America."

Tim Moraghan, the USGA championship agronomist, even went so far as to say that restoring Bethpage Black and taking the Open there was the most magnanimous gesture the organization has ever made.

This might have been a sweeping statement without Open contestants' collective perception that the USGA would have to strain to assemble a litany of good deeds. The players' vision is clouded by what they perceive to be the USGA's sadistic nature, even as they ignore their own masochistic tendencies that persuade them to gleefully return to the Open each year for more abuse.

The players nonetheless acknowledge that playing the Open on a municipal course is a good idea. This is the USGA's ultimate Open setup, understand. Taking the Open to a public course is a benevolent gesture, certainly, and one that on the eve of the Open will bring a feel-good quality to the championship.

The setup, among the most wickedly clever it has ever conceived, is this: The USGA, in its perennial quest to create a hell through which players are required to tiptoe, has asked Open contestants to play through a public park in the shadow of New York City.

Finally, the USGA has discovered the quintessential site for a mugging.